—THE—
DECOUPAGE
COLLECTION

THE
DECOUPAGE COLLECTION

MAGGIE PHILO

*New Ideas & Techniques
for Stylish Effects*

RIZZOLI
NEW YORK

First published in the United States of America in 1998 by
RIZZOLI INTERNATIONAL PUBLICATIONS, INC.
300 Park Avenue South, New York, NY 10010

First published in Great Britain in 1997 by
Aurum Press Ltd
25 Bedford Avenue
London WC1B 3AT

Design by Kit Johnson
Photographs by David Johnson

ISBN 0-8478-2094-7
LC   97-75703

Typeset by Dorchester Typesetting Group Ltd
Printed in Hong Kong by South China Printing Co. Ltd

CONTENTS

INTRODUCTION

Some years ago, not having lifted a pencil since I left school, I decided to attend a part-time art course at my local polytechnic. Students were expected to develop a style to their work, but I could never decide what my style might be. I would be influenced by Matisse, Kandinsky, Georgia O'Keeffe or Howard Hodgkin one day and Cézanne or Bonnard the next, and I hadn't, of course, the benefit of their talent. Having my fifth child partway through the course made it impossible for me to complete more than the minimum amount of work required. Although I learned a good deal about colour, tone and composition, I left without having built up any real confidence in my drawing or painting skills. Découpage was an absolutely brilliant discovery for me.

Now, I can be almost anyone I like and adopt whatever style I choose, to create three-dimensional works of art that I could only have dreamt of achieving previously. I can draw upon the skills of eighteenth- and nineteenth-century artists such as Redouté, Hooker or Sowerby, or use the wonderfully inventive designs of some contemporary artists. I know that découpage will appeal to many creative people who lack confidence to paint and draw free-hand, and I hope this book will also be of interest to more accomplished artists who want to extend their creative range in exciting directions.

The term découpage comes from the French word *découper*, meaning 'to cut'. The process involves cutting out a printed image and applying it to a surface. Usually, several coats of varnish are applied over the image so that it becomes an integral part of the surface. Until relatively recently, when I was asked what I did, the answer was inevitably followed by the question, 'what's that?' Now, I am pleased to say the tables have turned and it is often assumed that beautifully hand-painted items have been découpaged, much to the annoyance of the artists themselves. Découpage has, in fact, been around

quite some time. It was widely practised by the Venetians during the eighteenth century, to imitate oriental lacquerwork, which was so popular at the time that demand exceeded supply. It was known as *l'arte del povero*, or poor man's art. The fashion soon spread to France, where it was a favourite pastime among wealthy ladies of the French Court, and later to England, where it was hugely popular during Victorian times. Découpage all but died out by the beginning of the twentieth century, but resurfaced after the Second World War, when an American, Hiram Manning, and his mother Maybelle became interested in the craft after discovering some original French examples. Hiram Manning later wrote a book called *Manning on Découpage* (Dover Publications, available from addresses listed at the end of this book). It is a fascinating work containing the history of découpage as well as photographs of many exquisite examples and practical advice. Some of this is at odds with the information in my book, as I have been able to take advantage of the more user-friendly, water-based products now available. I have also adopted a simpler and more accessible approach, to suit the busy lives of people today.

Découpage is currently enjoying a huge revival. Not only do we have many historical images that were used by our predecessors, but also an endless variety of cheap and beautiful giftwraps, making poor man's art a rather apt name. With the constant flow of changing styles that are now produced, there is no reason for découpage ever to go out of fashion. Modern wrapping paper is often so well designed that much of it, I now feel, is too good to be torn off a gift and discarded. In this book I have explored many of the creative possibilities that découpage can offer and I hope that readers will feel encouraged to develop their own ideas. I have used many different examples of printed designs, from classical to contemporary, and experimented extensively with the range of technical possibilities opened up by modern photocopiers. Use of colour, paint effects and metal leaf all play an important part in creating a new look for découpaged projects as well as contributing to more familiar styles. So, whether you are a complete beginner or a découpage expert, a traditionalist or someone looking for a new direction, I hope this book will inspire you.

MAGGIE PHILO

PAPERS AND SURFACES

One of the most delightful aspects of découpage is that it can be used to transform almost any rigid surface, and this provides a wonderful variety of projects from which to choose. In this book you will find, as you would expect, items made from wood, metal and compressed fibreboard, but you will also see designs worked very successfully on the more unusual surfaces of ceramic, glass, paper and fabric. You will need to put together a basic materials kit to complete most of the projects and, of course, some inspiring decorative papers. You can choose from giftwrap, postcards and prints, books, magazines or Victorian scraps.

Paper sources

To make the most of the wide choice of papers available, you need access to suitable shops. The range available by mail-order is very limited, and, although friends can keep a look out for designs for you, discovering your own and imagining how you will interpret them is surely one of the most exciting and enjoyable aspects of this craft.

Giftwrap is probably the most accessible source of paper for découpage. It gives you the opportunity to work in a wide range of styles, as you can find anything from the beautifully illustrated Dutch flower paintings of the eighteenth century to the bold and colourful designs of contemporary artists. Look at the giftwrap in good department stores and stationery shops, bookshops, gift shops, galleries and museums. You will soon find it almost impossible to walk past a display without having a quick look! The quality of wrapping paper does vary considerably, however, some being rather thin. Thin paper makes the gluing process a bit more difficult, especially when handling larger pieces, so it is best to choose a good-quality paper with a simple design for your first projects.

Victorian scraps first appeared soon after the colour printing process was developed during the nineteenth century. They were produced in sheets which were beautifully embossed and die-cut, so that the need to cut out the image was virtually redundant. The images depicted were hugely sentimental and romantic with pictures of cherubs, fashionable ladies, fans, prettily dressed children, birds, pets, and so on. These scraps were used to decorate all manner of things and

collections were pasted into albums or 'scrap books'. These designs are still produced in much the same way today. However, the cost of die-cutting as accurately as in Victorian times would make them extremely expensive and so the need for careful cutting out has returned. If you cannot obtain these Victorian scraps locally, they are available by mail-order.

Books are another extremely useful source of printed material. I like to browse around those book shops that sell remaindered or damaged books at bargain prices and I now have a collection of more than a hundred books, including many with beautiful botanical illustrations. I normally buy at least two copies of a book I like, one for chopping up and one to keep. The logic behind this is that it is much cheaper to cut out the pages from a book than it is to colour-photocopy them, but should I want to repeat a design in the future, I still have the second book to photocopy from as often as I need. I have come across many people who are horrified at the thought of destroying a book, but if you keep the economics firmly in mind it won't seem half so bad and once you have made the first cut, you will soon become quite uninhibited!

Postcards and prints intended for framing can be used, although both are rather thick. Postcards can usually be thinned fairly easily by putting your thumbnail between the printed surface and the backing paper and carefully peeling them apart. Pull slowly to avoid tearing.

Thick paper is a little more difficult and time-consuming. You will need to press a damp sponge over the back of the print until the water has penetrated the paper but not soaked it. Then carefully peel away the surface of the paper with your fingertips bit by bit. The main drawback to this technique is that you can peel away too much and end up with a hole or tear in the paper which usually renders it unusable and certainly makes me want to scream. For this reason, I generally prefer to disguise the thickness of paper by applying a few more coats of varnish to my chosen project instead.

Black-and-white prints covering every subject imaginable can be found in copyright-free design books which you can obtain by mail-order or through your local bookshop. Most of these books contain designs from historic sources. Some are produced especially for découpage and contain a wide range of material including ornamental designs and borders. Since black-and-white photocopying is very inexpensive and accessible, these books provide a very practical and economical source of prints for découpage. They also have the advantage of being very versatile as the photocopies can be stained with tea so that they resemble old parchment, or painted with watercolours to create coloured prints. During the eighteenth century, when découpage was a popular pastime with wealthy ladies of the French and Italian courts,

black-and-white prints were produced by many well-known artists of the time to meet the need for suitable designs. These would be hand-coloured, pasted on to furniture and then given thirty or forty coats of varnish so that the finished piece resembled the oriental lacquerwork that was so fashionable during this period.

About the same time, print rooms were becoming popular in Britain. Prints would be collected, pasted directly on to a wall and surrounded by paper borders, swags and so on. You can still buy reproductions of these border designs – you will find a list of suppliers at the end of this book. You can use them to produce stylish, classical découpaged pieces and they are especially useful for decorating larger items of furniture such as screens.

Magazines can be used for decoration if the paper is of a reasonable quality, but newspaper pictures are generally unsuitable as the printing on the reverse tends to show through. It is better to make photocopies of very thin paper and also of photographs.

Copyright infringement need not concern you if you are making things for yourself and to give to friends. However, if you intend to sell your work you should not photocopy material unless it is free of copyright.

As I see it, if you are buying and cutting out a giftwrap, you are using rather than copying something. However, I would not like to comment on the legal implications which may vary across the world. Some manufacturers are quite happy for their papers to be used in this way while others are definitely not. Those who disapprove view it as others gaining commercially from

their designs. I have every sympathy with that point of view; when a giftwrap has been designed by a contemporary artist, I feel it is best to seek the approval of the supplier before using the design in your work.

Items to decorate

You will probably find you need look no further than around your own home for suitable items to start on. Most of us have a collection of either well-worn 'old friends' or ghastly new ones that can be transformed with a lick of paint and some nice paper. Packaging costs nothing and biscuit tins, tea caddies, Camembert boxes or tubular card containers (like those used for stacking crisps) are all ideal to practise on. Try to pick items that have a good flat surface without too many lumps or ridges.

Looking further afield, junk shops and rummage sales can provide all kinds of interesting finds. Old French enamelware and plain but interestingly shaped furniture are particularly worth seeking out. The condition of these items doesn't really matter as repairs can be hidden beneath paint and paper, whilst the odd dent or chip can only add to the aged and worn appearance that is so popular today.

Unfortunately there are few stores where you can buy a wide range of new undecorated items. The Swedish furnishing chain, Ikea, is the best that I have come across and its prices are extremely reasonable. However, try looking in home furnishing and department stores for paper shades, tin and ceramic containers, wooden frames, glassware, wastebins and trays. Garden centres are good for galvanized watering cans, planters and flower pots. DIY stores, gift, craft and stationery shops are also worth visiting for unusual boxes and penholders.

If you do not have a good supply of shops near you, or you simply can't face all the trekking around, then mail-order is the answer. There are a good many mail-order suppliers offering wooden, fibreboard and papier mâché items especially for decorating – a list is provided at the back of this book.

Preparation of surfaces

This is definitely not my favourite part of the découpage process, but the preparation of surfaces is often very important. I do not believe in creating unnecessary work, and not all surfaces need special treatment. However, it is important that all surfaces are clean and grease-free to ensure good adhesion of paint and papers. A smooth surface is always necessary and, whilst sandpaper is perfectly adequate, I used a small electric sander for many of the projects in this book and found it produced a very smooth surface in no time at all. I bought one with a triangular head that was good at getting right into corners, even on small projects.

There is a wide variety of paper backgrounds you can use for découpage, including photocopies, print room borders and decorative wrapping paper, which is available in countless styles featuring an enormous range of images from fruit, flowers and animals to classical motifs. You can découpage a range of different surfaces and objects, including galvanized metal, glass, terracotta, wood and papier mâché.

NEW WOOD

You should normally seal new wood either with clear shellac sanding sealer or an acrylic wood primer. However, I have found that this is not really necessary when painting smaller items that are made from good quality wood without knots. Start by filling any holes or cracks with a wood filler then sand the surface using a medium-grade sandpaper. Next, brush on the shellac or acrylic wood primer, following the manufacturer's instructions. If you have used the acrylic primer, you will need to sand the article lightly again before painting.

OLD WOOD

Previously painted or varnished wood needs to be cleaned thoroughly with warm soapy water and a cloth or brush. When it has dried, fill any holes and cracks with wood filler, then sand the surface well with a coarse-grade paper. This is necessary to achieve a surface to which paint will adhere. A highly-lacquered surface will need a considerable amount of sanding, and an electric sander is particularly useful here. Previously polished wood should be rubbed down with 00-grade steel wool dipped in methylated spirit to remove the polish, then sanded with a medium-grade paper when it is dry.

COMPRESSED FIBREBOARD

Compressed fibreboard is rather like a fine-textured chipboard. It is often used in place of wood as it is less expensive and easier to machine. Unfortunately, the machining process produces fine particles of dust which contain harmful glues, so, because of this, compressed fibreboard has been banned in some countries. The end product is perfectly safe, however, but if you machine it

yourself, do make sure you wear an appropriate face mask to protect against dust inhalation.

Good quality fibreboard needs no preparation and is an ideal surface for découpage as it is flat and even. Occasionally you may come across a poorer-quality product, where the surface roughens when you apply paint. If this happens, leave the paint to dry, then sand the surface smooth and treat as new wood by brushing on an acrylic primer. I should add that this has only happened to me once.

TIN AND GALVANIZED METAL

Clean all metal with warm soapy water to remove any traces of grease and dirt. Paint tin with a metal primer, following the manufacturer's instructions. It is now possible to buy a water-based metal primer and this is my preferred choice.

Occasionally, you may experience problems with adhesion. If you do, a drop or two of dish soap added to the paint usually puts this right. Both oil- and water-based primers dry to a matt finish and you can then use water-based latex paint over them.

New galvanized metal can be treated in the same way, but, providing it has not been coated with a metal lacquer, you can use a liquid primer sold specifically for the purpose. Brush the watery primer on to the surface, where it will turn black. Leave to dry, then clean off thoroughly using warm soapy water. I always choose this method for new galvanized metal because when latex paint is applied over this, it takes on a sort of pitted and textured appearance that I find very attractive (see Orchids watering can featured on page 97).

Old, weathered galvanized metal needs no preparation apart from thorough cleaning, unless there are

signs of rust. If this is the case, treat as old enamel.

ENAMEL

Old enamel nearly always shows traces of rust. Use a wire brush or coarse-grade sandpaper to remove any loose and flaking metal, then treat with a rust-proofing agent before applying an oil-based metal primer, or painting with an all-in-one rust proofer and primer. You will need to follow the manufacturer's instructions in either case. New enamel should be primed with an oil-based metal primer. Water-based metal primers do not adhere well to enamel surfaces.

PAPIER MÂCHÉ, PAPER AND CARD

Papier mâché and card need no special treatment, and emulsion paint can be applied directly to the surface. If you want a less absorbent surface, you can seal it with a coat of shellac. Paper surfaces do not need sealing before decorating with paper cutouts.

CERAMICS AND GLASS

Unglazed terracotta needs no special treatment and can be painted directly with latex paint. Glazed ceramics are best left unpainted, although it is possible to buy a tile primer and paint them if you are determined. Glass needs to be cleaned thoroughly in warm soapy water and polished with a lint-free cloth when dry.

FABRIC

Seal fabric with white glue. Use the same glue for sticking on the paper cutouts and for sealing the completed design. This will avoid patchy results.

GETTING STARTED

There are a number of things that you will need in order to get started and most of these can be found fairly easily in your local art shop and DIY store. If you have difficulty finding a product locally, there is a list of retailers who supply by mail-order at the end of the book. There are additional processes that can be combined with découpage, such as gilding and painted effects, which require other materials. Information on these is included in the relevant sections. Although découpage is not a difficult craft, it is a good idea to start with fairly simple projects and then move on to the more complicated ones when you feel confident that you are using the right amount of glue, are able to smooth away air bubbles easily and can accomplish trouble-free varnishing.

Materials

PREPARATION

Medium- and coarse-grade sandpaper are required to prepare most surfaces.

Primer may also be required to seal a surface (see page 12).

PAINTING

Water-based paint has been used for all the painted projects in this book, which means you can simply clean your brushes with water. You can choose from standard latex paint or from one of the traditional paint ranges now on the market. The traditional paints have a chalky-based texture and are based on natural rather than synthetic pigments. I love the quality and softness of colour that these paints have and use them most of the time. However, this paint is quite soft and easily marked, and if you try to retouch a spoilt area of paint, it leaves a watermark that is hard to disguise later.

Fine-grade sandpaper is required if you need to smooth any lumpy or uneven paint surfaces.

SEALING PAPER

Clear shellac is used to seal all types of paper before cutting out, apart from Victorian scraps which are already sealed with a lacquer. Pale French polish and shellac sanding sealer are both suitable and are much the same.

CUTTING

Scissors for cutting out your designs should be small, pointed and really sharp to achieve the level of accuracy required for good-quality work. I find straight-sided manicure scissors are best for this, but some people prefer curved scissors. It is a good idea to use whatever you find easiest and most comfortable.

A scalpel or **craft knife** is needed for cutting out delicate internal areas of a design; it is also useful for cutting straight lines such as borders.

A cutting mat is needed to protect your work surface when using a scalpel or craft knife. The best sort is a self-healing cutting mat which you can buy in art and craft shops. The smallest size ($8\frac{1}{2} \times 11$ in) mat is big enough for most purposes. You can use a piece of thick card as an alternative.

GLUING

Paste glue (such as wallpaper paste) is the easiest type to use when sticking on to a painted surface. It is relatively slow-drying and not too sticky, allowing extra time to reposition a motif and smooth out bubbles of air.

White glue (Sobo, Elmers Glue-All) has the extra transparency required when sticking paper on to glass and the adhesion required for gluing on to ceramics, fabrics or metal.

Repositional adhesive in spray or stick form is a temporary adhesive. It is necessary when arranging cutouts on a vertical surface, so that the elements of the design can be moved about until you have an arrangement that you like. It is also useful on a flat surface to keep in place a design that has several components, enabling you to glue them in place accurately.

A household sponge is needed to clean off the excess glue after you have stuck down your design.

A lino printing roller is not essential but is very useful for smoothing down paper inside trays and large flat surfaces.

VARNISH AND ABRASIVES

Satin acrylic varnish is used to build up the layers of varnish in the découpage process. This is water-based and brushes should be cleaned in water. Acrylic floor varnish is worth looking out for as it provides a very tough finish. It is usually a little thinner and more free-flowing, giving a lovely smooth surface to trays and other flat surfaces, but making it more likely to run on vertical ones, where you need to watch out for drips.

Matt acrylic varnish is nice to use for the last layer or two to make your finished project less shiny. It is not usually clear enough to use for more than three or four coats.

Sandpaper in 400 and 600 grit is needed to smooth out final layers of varnish. This does not scratch the surface as much as coarse sandpaper does. You will not need it if you are choosing an aged or antique look.

BRUSHES

Household paint brushes in 2.5 cm (1 in) and 4 cm (1¹/₂ in) sizes are suitable for most projects.

Flat varnish brushes are the best to use when applying varnish. I also use them for painting smaller items. You can buy them from art shops or specialist paint suppliers.

The tools and materials required for découpage (left) include: scissors, scalpel, cutting mat, mineral spirits, repositional spray adhesive, clear shellac, paste glue, lino printing roller, brushes for painting, gluing and varnishing, paint, sponge, ruler, acrylic varnish, sandpaper and finishing paper.

A brush for gluing. I use an inexpensive flat hog brush, like those generally used for oil-painting, for applying glue.

SUNDRIES

A lead pencil for disguising white edges of paper.

Paper towels for applying shellac to seal paper and for mopping up.

Mineral spirits or naphtha for cleaning up shellac.

A ruler for centring designs and mitring corners.

Techniques

DESIGN AND COLOUR

Having settled on a project and prepared the surface, the next step is to choose your paper design and paint colour. It is usually best to decide on the paper first then choose a background colour that works well with it. However, you can work the other way round if, for instance, you want to paint your article to match a specific colour scheme.

I keep pieces of lining paper, each approximately 15 cm (6 in) square, painted with all the colours I own, in order to hold them against the paper I want to use. This throws up some interesting ideas and combinations of colour and gives a far better idea than the minute colour samples that manufacturers provide. I do have the advantage of an extensive colour range which, if you are a beginner, you won't have, but you can still get ideas by holding your chosen paper against any source of colour you have around you – in books or on walls, fabric or household items.

When making your choice of paper, you will need to bear in mind the shape and proportions of the item to be decorated. For instance, a botanical painting of a single flower stem looks very good on a tall narrow item such as a flower bucket, but would look wrong in the middle of a rectangular tray. A round surface is enhanced by using a circular design.

PAINTING

You will always need to use at least two coats of paint for your project, even if one gives a good coverage, as it is possible that some of the paint may be removed when you are cleaning off excess glue. Many people tend to paint in neat, even lines, which is not necessary or even desirable, if you want to create an antiqued effect. I would recommend that wooden items be painted in the direction of the grain of the wood, with the exception of circular objects, but other surfaces can be painted randomly. In any case, most of the brush marks will eventually disappear beneath layers of varnish.

If you are going to use the antiquing glaze described on page 30, the marks left by your paint brush are integral to the process so keep this in mind when applying paint; do not smooth them away.

SEALING THE PAPER

With the exception of Victorian scraps, all paper needs to be sealed on the printed side. This is done by applying clear shellac to the surface with paper towels. The shellac dries within a few minutes, becoming invisible, and the paper will be strengthened and water-resistant. This is important as it protects the surface from damage during the gluing process. You will also have the benefit of a cleaner cutting edge after sealing the paper with shellac.

If you are using only part of a sheet of giftwrap or other paper, separate the area you require from the rest and seal that portion only.

CUTTING

Cutting out is one of the most important parts of the découpage process and the quality of your work will depend on it. Unfortunately, I have too often seen what would have otherwise been a good project let down by poor and hurried cutting. This always seems a shame to me as I find cutting out both relaxing and therapeutic and one of the most enjoyable aspects of the craft. Choose a comfortable chair, turn on some music or listen to the radio and take your time.

You should start by roughly cutting around the required motif to remove excess paper. Next, using the scalpel knife and cutting mat, cut out the delicate enclosed areas of the design, if there are any. This should be done before the remainder is cut out because it is very difficult to do without damaging the cutout when you are handling a flimsy structure. When using a scalpel knife, you need to press down firmly as you cut. Insufficient pressure can result in damaging and tearing the paper, particularly if the blade is not absolutely razor-sharp.

Using a sharp pair of manicure scissors, cut out the remainder of the design, working just on or inside the edge and moving the paper towards the scissors as you go. You should try not to leave any of the white edge of the paper showing.

Sometimes, as when a motif includes delicate detail, such as the antennae of a butterfly or the leg of an insect, this is impossible. In such a case, cut the section very slightly wider and fill it in with pencil or colour after you have glued the motif in place. If these parts are

amputated by mistake, you can always reinstate them by drawing them in. Don't worry if you make a cut too long and separate a section of a motif from the rest. All pieces can be joined together easily at the gluing stage.

Cut out enclosed areas with a scalpel; use scissors for remainder.

Mitre borders with a ruler and scalpel.

Mitring borders When you are using borders, you may need to mitre corners. This is not done at the cutting-out stage but during the gluing process. The border should be cut a little longer than is needed. If it has a strong pattern, it may be necessary to centre each section to get a neat result. Stick most of the border in place, leaving the last inch or two unglued and overlapping. If possible, take a metal ruler that is long enough to lay across your design and reach opposite corners. Then cut across the angles with a scalpel. If you don't have a long enough metal ruler, use a straight edge or any other ruler, mark the angle with a pencil, and then cut through this line. You may find with narrow borders you can simply mark the angle with a pencil by eye before cutting through it.

Curving borders You can curve a straight border by making a series of little cuts at regular intervals partway through the width of the border. This enables you to ease it into position, overlapping the little cut sections on the inside of the curve. With very narrow borders on a gently curved surface, you can usually ease the paper into place without cutting.

ARRANGING THE DESIGN

If you are planning a design that consists of several motifs, it is a good idea to cut more pieces than you think you are going to need. This gives the opportunity to play around with the design, trying out different arrangements. Even after making several hundred projects, I cannot look at a blank object and a sheet of designs and decide precisely which elements I will need, so I now have quite a large box of surplus cutouts to draw upon from time to time. This is really the fun part of découpage, so enjoy yourself and experiment!

The overall balance of a design is important and on certain items where the arrangement is not evenly spread, it is better to put the weight at the bottom rather than at the top. The spaces in between the motifs are a very important part of the design and should be looked at carefully. You can use a small motif, such as a butterfly or insect, to fill a gap if necessary and to give balance to the whole. A design doesn't necessarily have to be symmetrical, and it can sometimes look a little boring if it is, but symmetry is certainly useful for some projects, making the designing job easier and giving a balance that might not otherwise be there. I have in mind the glass fruit plate on page 76, the striped hat box on page 50, where the design is repeated on opposite halves of the item, and the chess board on page 132, where two sides are decorated differently with opposite sides more or less matching.

Arranging cutouts on a flat surface is fairly straightforward, as the pieces of paper should stay where you put them. Even so, when you have decided on an arrangement that you like, it is a good idea to fix it in place temporarily with repositionable glue. This not only prevents accidents where children and pets 're-arrange' your design, it also enables you to glue the cutouts in the correct position more accurately. This is particularly true with an overlapping arrangement.

When working on a vertical surface, unless it is a very simple design with only one or two motifs, you really do need to hold the arrangement in place with repositionable adhesive before gluing it permanently in position.

GLUING

When I first tried my hand at découpage, I stuck down rather a large motif cut from thin wrapping paper, using white glue. The result was a lumpy crinkled mess. At the time, there were no helpful books that might have pointed to where I was going wrong, so I decided I was using the wrong glue and instead tried a simple starch paste glue for paper (wallpaper paste). Success!

There are now, of course, quite a number of books on découpage, and nearly all recommend white glue. I have to take my hat off to the authors of these because I think it is much more difficult to use this type of glue as it dries so fast; you can slow the drying process down a bit, however, by diluting the glue with water.

Starch paste glue gives you a little more time to smooth out all bubbles of air and to reposition a motif if the placement is not quite right. You can mix up a small quantity of wallpaper paste instead of buying a ready-made glue, if you prefer, and it is similar to use. I recommend brushing the surface of the object with glue rather than the back of the cutout. This makes the process much less messy and the paper cutout will be easier to handle. It also means that you don't have to lift the whole print off the surface and risk gluing it back in the wrong position. Judging the right amount of glue to use may take a little practice. If you use too little, the motif may lift, too much and it will be difficult to clean off the excess.

You will need to wash the glue off your hands at intervals when gluing several motifs to keep your fingers from sticking to the paper and damaging the surface. If damage does occur during this process – perhaps you have forgotten to seal the paper with shellac – you can often disguise an area by retouching it with watercolour paints and re-sealing with shellac, or by using coloured pencils.

Start by removing a paper cutout or lifting a section of a larger motif, then brush glue on to the surface to cover an area slightly larger than the displaced print. Place the paper back into position and press down firmly with your fingertips, smoothing out all bubbles of air from the centre of the paper towards the edges. Continue in this way until all sections of the design have been glued in place. Examine your work under a good light to make sure that it is completely smooth and well stuck down, applying a dab of glue to any areas that are not.

Allow to dry for about half an hour, then clean off all the excess glue with a damp sponge. Failure to do this thoroughly can result in a patchy appearance beneath the varnish. Leave the item to dry for a further two hours at least. If you have an overlapping arrangement of motifs, you don't have to wait for one piece of paper to dry before laying another over it, as you might think, but you will need to take extra care and press very firmly over the underlying edges of paper so that you remove all traces of air.

When your design is dry, use a lead pencil to fill in and disguise any white edges and areas of paper that have been joined. This is also the time to repair a damaged surface with paint or coloured pencils and draw in any fine detail, such as chopped-off antennae or insect legs, using a very fine permanent black or sepia marker pen. Let the ink dry for at least half an hour. Finally, make sure that every edge of your design is stuck down properly before moving on to the next stage.

VARNISHING

Historically, thirty or forty coats of slow-drying oil-based varnish were applied to découpage work and each layer, apart from the first few, was smoothed with a fine abrasive. This means that it must have taken a month to complete a project!

Nowadays, we have water-based varnish which makes the process much easier and more pleasant. The varnish dries quickly and smoothly, before too many fibres and other debris have had time to settle on the surface and become embedded in it. This removes the necessity to sand between coats, apart from the last one or two, if you require a smooth finish. You should not sand at all unless you have at least six layers of varnish, or you will remove the printed edges of the cutout and the white paper beneath will be visible.

The découpaged flowerpot (below).

Try to work in a dust-free area when using varnish and, if possible, choose a room that is not used too frequently, where your projects can remain undisturbed behind a closed door.

Although the varnish dries quickly, before fibres have much of a chance to settle, it would be tempting fate to wear a mohair sweater while working, as would wearing a brand new outfit (I know!) because if a splash of varnish dries on your clothing, it is impossible to remove. It is best to avoid all woollen or fibrous clothing; a cotton shirt is ideal to work in.

The number of layers of varnish you apply is really a matter of choice, but between ten and twelve coats is a good number for most purposes. I personally feel that less

than three is a bit faint-hearted while more than twenty is going beyond the call of duty! Ten or twelve coats of varnish may seem rather a lot, but they actually take a very short time to apply.

When you are ready to start, think of the first two coats of varnish as sealing the paper rather than building up the varnish. These sealing layers need to be thin, as overwetting the surface at the start can cause the paper to lift and wrinkle. You should leave the varnish to dry for at least two hours between these and every subsequent layer of varnish, even if it feels dry earlier. Every manufacturer of the varnishes that I have used recommends this amount of time and the surface can be spoiled if you don't follow this advice.

All vertical surfaces need to be checked for drips about five minutes after the application of varnish, and the drips should be removed with a brush. Make sure that all flat surfaces are free of dust and fibre before applying further layers. Wipe the article with a damp sponge or dust with a lint-free cloth if you need to. Because the varnish appears milky when wet, it is possible that you may shed a hair on to the surface, which may not be visible until the varnish is dry. If this happens, the hair is usually quite easy to lift off with the point of a scalpel. After you have completed the first two thin coats, apply the varnish a little more thickly, but obviously not so thickly that it runs. To achieve a smooth finish, sand the surface with a fine-grade finishing paper and brush on a final coat of varnish (repeat for a better result). If you prefer a less shiny appearance, as I do, complete the varnishing process by using a matt varnish instead of a satin finish for the final two coats.

Step-by-Step Technique

This simple flower pot illustrates the basic techniques of découpage.

YOU WILL NEED

Flower pot

Paper motifs

Water-based paint

Satin acrylic varnish

Clear shellac

Paste glue

Manicure scissors

Lead pencil

Brushes for painting, gluing and varnishing

Damp sponge

Paper towels for applying shellac

Fine-grade finishing paper

Paint the flower pot with two coats of water-based paint (**1**), leaving the first coat to dry throughly before applying the second.

Seal the paper surface with a coat of shellac (**2**), then carefully cut out the design from the paper using manicure scissors.

Brush the glue on to the surface of the pot (**3**), then place the motif over the glue and press it firmly into position with your fingers. Carefully smooth out any bubbles of air trapped beneath the paper, working from the centre of the motif towards the edges of the paper. Leave to dry for half an hour.

Wash off the excess glue with a damp sponge (**4**) and leave to dry for a further two hours.

Fill in any white edges of paper with a lead pencil (**5**).

Apply six or more coats of satin acrylic varnish over the pot (**6**). Sand the surface smooth, then brush on a final layer of varnish.

1

2

3

4

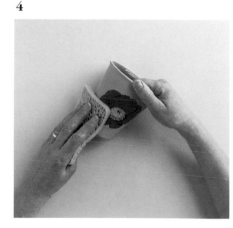

5

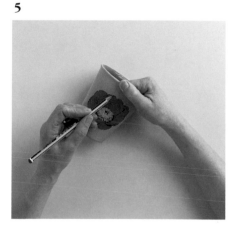

6

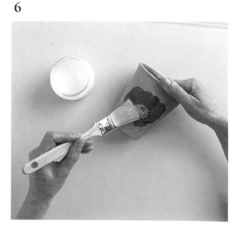

PAINT TECHNIQUES

A number of paint techniques have been used throughout this book and most are simple and fun to do. They are not an essential part of the découpage process, however, and many projects look just as effective with a plain background, allowing the papers to speak for themselves. I have kept most of the paint finishes very soft so that they subtly enhance a paper design rather than fight with it. Soft stripes seem to work surprisingly well, and if you want to give a plain background added interest you can always paint a contrasting border – very easy with the help of masking tape.

All the paint effects use water-based paint, either full strength or diluted, or acrylic gel medium mixed with colour. Acrylic gel medium is a transparent, slow-drying substance. It has a gel-like consistency which enables it to hold the marks made by brushes, sponges and other tools. You can colour it with artist's acrylic colour or add it to latex paint.

All techniques require a base of at least two coats of water-based paint.

If you are using gel medium, this basecoat should be satin latex paint or a matt paint sealed with acrylic varnish. There are no precise formulas for the paint/water or paint/gel mixes because they very much depend on the product you are using and the depth of colour you require. It is best to experiment before you begin; try out a chosen colour and practise a technique first on a piece of card or scrap of wood

sealed with varnish. To save repainting a project if you make a mistake or change your mind, seal your base colour with two coats of satin acrylic varnish and you will then be able to wipe off the subsequent colour easily with a damp cloth before it dries.

Paint-and-water glazes dry very quickly, but you should allow at least four hours for paint-and-gel mixes to dry.

Sponging

You will need a *natural sea sponge*, diluted *latex paint* or *paint-and-gel mix*, and a *plate* or *paint tray*.

Dip the sponge into the paint, wiping off the excess on the side of the tray or plate. Dab the sponge randomly over the surface, twisting your hand this way and that as you go. You can keep the sponging to a minimum to create a mildew effect, or build up the colour so that it almost obliterates the base colour.

Colour-washing

Stippled effect You will need a *dishcloth*, a *paintbrush*, *gel medium* and *colour*.

Brush the paint mix on to your surface using cross-hatched strokes. Make a pad with the dishcloth and dab this over the paint surface.

Colour-washing You will need a length of *dishcloth*, a *paintbrush* and some diluted *latex paint*.

Brush the paint roughly over the surface, then quickly wipe a pad of dishcloth over the wet paint, so that it blends in and brush marks are eliminated. Repeat this process with the same shade or a slightly different one. Three or four layers will give a depth of colour, and a final coat of very diluted white or off-white gives a subtle blended effect. Add a small amount of gel to the washes if you want to slow the drying time.

Use a sponge to obliterate a surface, or to create a mildew or stippled effect (left). Use a dishcloth to colourwash or create a stippled effect over light and dark surfaces (right).

You will need *water-based paint*, a *paintbrush*, 00-grade steel wool, either *fine-* or *medium-grade sandpaper*, *clear liquid wax* and a *small boar's hair brush*.

Use the brush to paint liquid wax over the surface in small patches, paying particular attention to areas where you would normally expect wear and tear such as corners and edges. Load the brush with more wax and, holding the brush over the surface, run a finger through the bristles in order to flick fine spots of wax on to the surface. Leave this to dry for at least half an hour, then paint on a contrasting colour.

When this is dry, remove the paint from the waxed areas by rubbing it with steel wool. A final rub with sandpaper will remove additional paint and wax. This finish gives an elegant, aged look to your project.

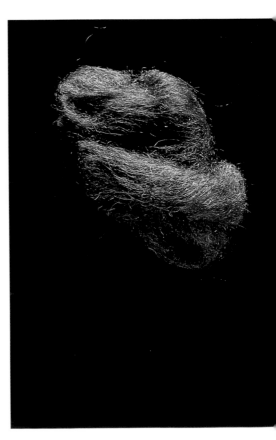

Dragging and stippling

Dragging You will need a *flat varnish brush* and *acrylic gel medium* tinted with *artist's acrylic paint*.

Keeping a steady hand, drag the gel mix across or down the painted surface as appropriate, using the varnish brush pressed almost flat against the surface. For a softer look, go over the same area again.

Stippling You will need a *stipple brush* for large areas, a *stencil brush* for corners and very small areas, and *acrylic gel medium* tinted with *artist's acrylic paint*.

Paint the gel mix on to the surface using cross-hatched strokes. Starting from one edge, progress towards the opposite one, pressing the brush on to the painted surface with a dabbing motion. The aim is to give an even distribution and texture to the glaze.

Dragging and stippling paint (above); distressing with sand and wax (right).

For a different effect, omit the wax application, and distress by using sandpaper to remove paint from some areas.

Painted borders

You will need *low-tack masking tape* for straight lines, *flexible masking tape* for curves, *paint* or *paint glaze* and a *narrow brush*.

Choose a masking tape the same width as you would like your painted border to be. Place a strip of tape around the edge of your project, in the position where you want the border. Place a second strip adjacent to this. Remove the first strip and paint the border using a contrasting colour and whatever technique is appropriate.

Painting borders using tape (right).

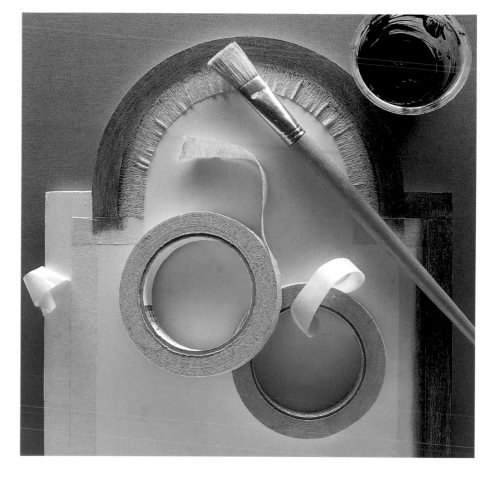

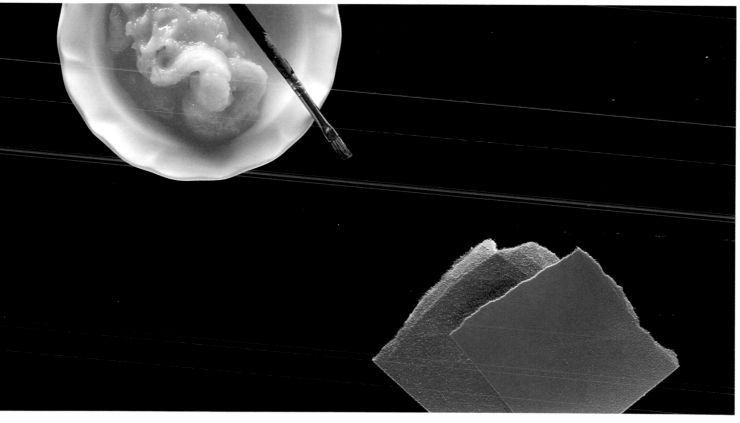

PAPER BACKGROUNDS

A paper surface for paper cutouts seems to me particularly appropriate. This medium can extend the creative possibilities of découpage and provide an exciting new direction in which to work. There are so many wonderful varieties of paper background – you can choose from handmade, marbled, textured and faked leather papers as well as all kinds of printed matter. Music books, newspapers and old documents can all be photocopied, and these can then be stained with tea so that the paper resembles old parchment (see page 27).

Rectangular or square shapes, such as boxes and books are the easiest to cover, and box-files make a very good and useful project as they are readily obtainable and inexpensive. You can use a large sheet of paper to cover the chosen object, or join smaller pieces together, disguising the seams with the découpage design.

Covering a Book Box

YOU WILL NEED

A book box

A sheet of paper big enough to cover the surface

Pencil and metal ruler

Scalpel and cutting mat or thick card

Paste glue and brush

Lino printing roller (optional)

Fold the paper around the box and, using a pencil, mark a rectangle big enough to cover both sides of the box and the spine, with a margin of 2.5 cm (1 in) all round. Lay the paper on a cutting mat or thick card and cut out the marked rectangle using the scalpel and a metal ruler. Draw a line down the centre of the back of the paper, where the spine will go.

Spread the glue evenly over the back of the paper and lay the middle of the spine over the line you have drawn on the paper. Press the paper on to the spine, smoothing away any air bubbles. Next, press each side of the paper against the sides of the box in turn. As you do so, make sure that you stretch the paper away from the spine and smooth out any bubbles of air towards the edges of the box (**1**). Use a lino printing roller to do this, if you have one, as it helps to give a firm even pressure over the surface.

Trim the paper from both ends of the spine and glue in place. Mitre the corners, allowing an extra 6 mm ($^1/_4$ in) or so to fold over edges (**2**). None of this needs to be too precise as all of the paper edges will be hidden beneath the strip that forms the false pages.

Measure and cut out three strips of paper to cover the sides of the box representing the edges of the 'pages'. Only the width matters at this stage. Glue one strip of paper in place and leave it to dry (**3**). Trim it to the correct length with a scalpel knife and glue the remaining strips in place in the same way.

Leave the box to dry before decorating it with your chosen motifs. The paper cover may crinkle a little when you glue on the paper cutouts, but this will shrink back in place when the glue dries.

1

2

3

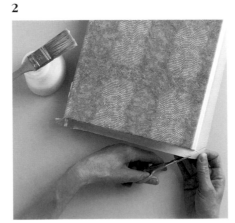

PHOTOCOPYING TECHNIQUES

Photocopying provides the obvious benefit of allowing you to copy a print instead of cutting up an original, and it also has a great many other creative uses. You can enlarge and reduce, alter colour and create mirror images. The black ink of a black-and-white copy can be replaced by any other single colour you choose and you can copy on to coloured paper. Transparent copies can be made by transferring the image on to varnish or by copying on to acetate. Colour prints can be turned into black-and-white ones, and these in turn can be hand-coloured or tinted with tea so that they resemble old parchment. Both acetate and paper copies can be gilded, giving découpage a completely new direction. All these techniques have been used on projects in this book.

The quality of photocopies can vary considerably. This is particularly true of colour copies where success is dependent on the copier used and its operator. These machines are complex and require an experienced and well-trained technician. Try to find a specialist copy shop that serves designers and architects.

Altered images

You can enlarge and reduce the size of your print accurately by following a simple formula. Measure the size you want your print to be, divide it by the size it is and multiply by 100. For example:

10 cm (4 in) divided by 20 cm (8 in) = 50% reduction.

20 cm (8 in) divided by 10 cm (4 in) = 200% enlargement.

I wasted so many copies guessing size incorrectly before this advice was given to me and I am extremely grateful for the money it has now saved me! It hardly needs pointing out that being able to create designs to fit a specific area is one of the most useful services a photocopier can provide.

Photocopiers can now do such wonderful things as repeating a

Photocopies of a Victorian rooster showing enlarged, reduced and reversed images.

single image across a page and creating a reverse image. Mirror images provide a very good way of giving a project balance, enabling two halves of a design to face one another. This is particularly useful if you want to decorate panels.

Coloured inks and papers

Some black-and-white copiers can print with a small range of coloured inks, to give, for example, a blue-and-white photocopy. With a true colour copier, however, almost any colour is possible (see *Remember Me* on page 137). It can also scan a colour sample and print in that colour. You can use any coloured paper in a black-and-white copier, but usually only cream or white paper in a colour copier.

Cream is a soft alternative to white and works particularly well when combined with a painted background in the same shade.

If you paint your background the same shade as your paper copy, whether this is white, cream or any other colour, you will not need to cut out all the internal areas of a motif; once varnished, they will be indistinguishable from the paint.

Sometimes you may come across a beautiful design that is too intricate to cut out. One way of getting around the problem is to paint the background the same colour as the paper you intend to use, but there are more ways to cheat than this!

DECALS

A decal is a printed image which has been transferred on to glossy acrylic varnish. Decal or transfer varnish is available from art shops. (There is a special medium made by Plaid called Picture This.) Roughly cut out your image, leaving a margin of at least 12 mm (1/2 in). Brush about six to eight coats of varnish over the printed surface of the photocopy, making sure each coat is dry before applying the next. A flimsy structure may need more coats to make it easier to handle. When the varnish is thoroughly dry, soak the photocopy in tepid water for twenty minutes or

more, then peel apart the paper and the plastic film on to which the ink has now been transferred. Lay the transfer on a flat surface to dry, then trim away the excess around the edges of the design with a sharp pair of manicure scissors.

Finally, glue the transfer into position on your surface using the same medium from which you made the decal, and continue by varnishing in the usual way. This technique needs a pale background colour to display it to best advantage, as tiny fibres of paper left in the varnish would show against a dark background. A pale cream colour works well, and you can use tinted glazes and varnish over the varnished decal to alter the shade.

COPYING ON TO ACETATE

This technique works absolutely brilliantly with découpage. The transparent images can be cut out and glued on to any surface except unpainted metal, glass and glazed porcelain. The glue needs to dry

completely transparently for this technique to be successful, however, and I have found that only white glue is sufficiently transparent, but this will not dry between two non-porous surfaces.

However, you can copy on to *self-adhesive acetate* and I have used this to decorate the star motif vase on page 58. The surface of the acetate was sealed with clear shellac before cutting out and the vase was transformed in an instant – no glue or varnish were required!

For me, the most exciting aspect of using an acetate image for découpage is that you can apply metal leaf to the back of it, thereby creating unusual and stunning effects. This is done very simply by following the basic gilding technique described on page 28.

Decal of photocopies before and after cutting out (below left), and photocopies on acetate (below right).

Tinting photocopies

TEA STAINING

The white paper of a photocopy can be made to resemble old parchment by staining with tea. Make a fairly strong brew with a tea bag in about a quarter of a cup of water, then simply wipe the bag over the printed surface. Add a little coffee to the mix if you like, or use it on its own and apply with a brush. I generally use a varnish brush to paint the tea on to large areas. If you want to add more colour, let the first application dry before you do so or the paper will become too wet and the printed surface will be damaged.

Leave the photocopy to dry before sealing with shellac and cutting out.

ADDING COLOUR

Black-and-white photocopies can be turned into brightly coloured prints by painting them with watercolour inks. This technique can give a very contemporary feel to a design, even when using historical material. You can also use watercolour or thinned gouache paints and, for a softer look, coloured pencils are good too. Colouring in a photocopy can be as simple or elaborate as you like, so choose a level that suits your ability.

When colouring a print simply, it is easy to imagine yourself back in nursery school, filling in blocks of colour and not minding when you smudge the edges. As you are going to cut the design out, this doesn't matter at all. You will probably find it easier at first to use two or three

Black-and-white photocopies stained with tea (left) and coloured with bright watercolour inks (right).

tones of a single colour, introducing more as you gain confidence. Shading is easier than you might think because you have the light and the dark areas in the print to guide you. Since photocopies are cheap and colour is applied before cutting out, you don't have to worry about spoiling anything and can afford to experiment with different techniques.

It is very important to remember to seal a painted photocopy with shellac before varnishing or you risk having the colour run into the varnish.

GILDING

*M*etal leaf has a lustrous quality that is not matched by paint and it can be used to create stunning effects when combined with découpage. If the gilding process sounds daunting to you, do not worry, the simple technique used in this book is very easy to master. Transfer metal leaf, acrylic gold size and a soft brush are all that you require to cover paint, card, glass, acetate and paper, and the basic technique for all these surfaces is exactly the same. For a quick and softer touch of gold on the edges, simply rub a little gilt cream over the surface with your finger.

Transfer metal leaf comes in packs of 25 squares, with a waxed paper backing for transferring it to a surface. Each sheet consists of finely-beaten metal and although you can buy real gold and silver leaf, bronze, aluminum, and copper leaf are good substitutes. These are much less expensive than gold and silver leaf, and just as effective when used for decorative techniques beneath varnish. The metal leaf is best cut into strips for gilding small areas.

Acrylic gold size is a water-based size to which the metal leaf adheres. It has a milky appearance when brushed on to a surface but becomes transparent very quickly. It is best to use a soft synthetic flat-bristled brush for applying the size so as to leave as few brush marks as possible. These can show beneath the leaf and make the finished appearance less attractive. After applying, the size is ready to gild over in about fifteen minutes, but it will stay tacky indefinitely, so it can be left longer if necessary. Large areas will need to be worked fairly quickly, because if you over-brush an area that has started to dry, you will disturb the surface and it will become lumpy.

Gilt creams have a less lustrous quality than leaf and are used over the varnish to complete a project. They can be applied evenly over a surface, but if you require an aged effect, try a more patchy application, so that the paint colour beneath shows through.

Gilt creams are a mix of finely ground metal powder and wax. A wide choice of colours is available and they can be applied with a brush or finger. You could also use a Q-tip. When the cream is dry, after about 24 hours, buff with a soft cloth to create a soft sheen.

Step-by-Step Gilding

YOU WILL NEED

Surface for gilding
Transfer metal leaf
Acrylic gold size
Soft-haired synthetic brush
Cotton ball

Paint the size on to the surface using the soft synthetic brush and leave for about fifteen minutes until it has become transparent (**1**).

Lay the sheet of metal in position over the size and gently press it into place with your fingertips. Then remove the paper backing sheet (**2**).

Smooth the leaf down gently, using a cotton ball (**3**).

1

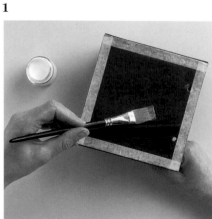

2

3

AGEING TECHNIQUES

A n aged look for découpaged items is enormously popular, and as many of the papers used are reproductions of historic paintings and designs, this works extremely well. One approach is to use a paint-finish surface beneath the découpage, but there are a number of other techniques for ageing your work which are applied on top of the découpage surface. These range from the simple application of an ageing wax to brushing with a tinted glaze or using the slightly trickier cracking varnishes. Serious-minded devotees of this look can combine all these techniques, but take care not to obliterate your beautifully cut-out designs completely, unless of course you have something to hide. Ageing can be a very good way of concealing mistakes!

There are certain advantages to making your découpaged items look old. Paint and varnish need not be absolutely smooth; a few lumps and bumps all add to the effect. A damaged paper surface is much less noticeable, and dust and fibres get lost among all the fake dirt that you apply. If you live in a house with animals and children and work on the kitchen table, this is definitely the look for you!

Antiquing paint

Many of the projects in this book have been painted with a watery raw umber paint which is applied after the second layer of varnish has dried and the surface is completely sealed. The basic recipe is:

1 part white latex paint
3 parts raw umber powdered pigment
8 parts water

The amount of water may need to be adjusted slightly to suit your taste and according to the quality of paint and pigment used.

Brush the paint on to the varnished surface. A minute or so later, before the paint starts to look

dry, clean it off the surface with a dry piece of paper towel. You will see that the paint is left behind in corners, brush marks and other places where dirt would collect. The surface over the cutout will have only slight brush marks from the varnish, thus holding less of the paint, but this doesn't seem to matter. You can rub less hard here or dab a little paint on with a damp

sponge if you like. To get an even result, work on only one surface of your item at a time – if it is a large piece, you will need to work quickly. Don't worry, though, if the result is not to your liking, or is a total disaster, you can simply wash it off and start again!

Antiquing over straight brush strokes (below right), and cross-hatched strokes (left).

Craquelure

This technique is used after all the layers of varnish have been applied. There are some new water-based, two-part craquelure kits now available. Instructions vary and you will need to follow each individual manufacturer's advice. Apart from the projects on pages 89 and 115 where I have used my own water-based recipe described on page 88, I have used an oil-and-water-based craquelure kit for all the projects in this book. This consists of a slow-drying oil-based varnish followed by a quick-drying water-soluble one. An oil paint is rubbed into the resulting cracked surface so that the cracks become visible. An oil-based varnish is finally applied to seal the surface. Raw umber paint is good for producing an aged look, but any colour can be used.

This technique has a fascination all of its own and, judging from the correspondence I receive, getting it right seems to be the preoccupation of many! Unfortunately, the manufacturers of these two-part varnishes do not provide very comprehensive information, and, as good results and drying times are dependent on weather conditions, which of course vary, the results are never quite predictable. However, the following advice should help.

Avoid using this technique on a wet day, or on a cold one in a room without heating. In both cases, cracks are unlikely to appear without directing a heat source to the varnished surface and this doesn't always produce a cracking as attractive and even as that which occurs naturally. If a warm and sunny day suddenly turns cold and wet, you may have to apply some heat. Placing the item in an airing cupboard or holding it near a light bulb is often sufficient. You can use a hair dryer but make sure it is held at some distance from the surface on a gentle setting, otherwise an unnatural-looking crazing will occur. In winter, a radiator is usually the answer. Most of the crackled projects in this book needed to be completed during a cold and rainy September

Raw umber paint rubbed into cracks.

before the central heating would normally be turned on in our house. Publishing schedules couldn't wait, so, in sheer frustration, I switched on the radiator, peeled off layers of clothing and relaxed, knowing I would get perfect results. My projects were placed in my favourite place on the kitchen table next to the radiator with its unbroken record of reliability!

The size of the cracks is dependent on the thickness of both layers of varnish and the length of time between applying them. Thicker coats of varnish and a shorter time between applications produces larger cracks. Larger items are best worked a section at a time, otherwise they become too difficult to handle. If you do not like the result, you can clean the varnishes off quite easily by simply washing away the water-based one and removing the oil-based layer with mineral spirits. Because the second varnish is water-soluble, you must take care not to wet the surface or handle your project with damp or clammy hands until it has been finally sealed.

YOU WILL NEED

2-part oil-and-water-based crackle kit
Boar brush for applying oil varnish
Soft-haired synthetic brush for applying water varnish
Raw umber artist's oil paint
Oil-based varnish and brush
Mineral spirits
Paper towels

Brush the oil-based varnish evenly over the surface of your design. Leave this to dry for between two and four hours, until it feels dry when you glide the back of your finger over the surface, but is still just tacky when you press your knuckle on to it. Brush on the water-soluble varnish, using a soft-haired synthetic brush so as to eliminate brush marks. Make sure every part of the first varnish is covered.

After about half an hour, this varnish should be dry and the surface cracked. Check to see if there are any areas that are not covered with the water varnish, touch them in and leave to dry. Any areas that are missed will result in a dark patch at the next stage. You may need to hold your item up to a good light for the cracks to be apparent. If cracking has not occurred, leave the article in a warm place until it does, or apply a gentle heat. Dilute some raw umber artist's oil paint with a little mineral spirit so that it has a creamy texture and rub this on to the surface, using a piece of paper towel. Take a clean piece of paper towel and wipe it off, leaving the paint remaining in the cracks. If you do have any unwanted

dark patches, they can be removed to some extent with a dab of mineral spirit. Leave the item to dry overnight, then seal it with an oil-based varnish.

Using coloured waxes

Wax can be applied over varnish and this is done once all the layers have been completed. The last coat of varnish needs to be matt because wax does not adhere well to a shiny surface. If you want to apply wax over a crackled surface, use a matt oil-based varnish to seal the water-soluble varnish. I very often complete a découpaged project with wax because it gives a quality and feel to the piece which is quite

Antiquing with brown wax (above).

unlike that of varnish. You can use a clear wax if you don't want to age or alter the colour of your work.

The coloured waxes normally used for staining and polishing wood are the ones to buy. The colours range from yellowing waxes for antiquing pine, neutral browns intended for oak and walnut to the red browns used on mahogany.

Yellow waxes look lovely over green, white, cream or yellow shades, but they make all blue paint look green. The mid- to dark-brown tones work well over all colours. Apply the wax with a piece of paper towel or soft cloth, rubbing in well. Leave it for half an hour or so, then polish to a soft shine.

DÉCOUPAGE UNDER GLASS

Découpage under glass was popular in the eighteenth and nineteenth centuries and was used in particular for decorating vases so that they resembled fine porcelain. The technique was known by the extremely odd-sounding name of 'portichomania'. The glass surface replaces the layers of varnish and the process is largely done in reverse, with the front of the paper glued to the glass, the paint applied to the back of the paper, and so on. In fairness, I should point out that the time saved in applying the layers of varnish probably does not equal the extra time spent on arranging the design and being painstakingly careful in gluing it in place.

Absolutely stunning results can be achieved by applying découpage under glass and the technique can be combined successfully with others, such as gilding or craquelure, to produce a wide range of stylish designs. These additional processes will again need to be reversed, with the metal leaf being applied after the paper, and the craquelure being applied directly to the glass surface before anything else.

If choosing a glass vase to decorate, it is best to select one with a fairly narrow top so that, when decorated, not too much of the painted surface inside will be visible. However, the neck cannot be so narrow that you are unable to put your hand inside to decorate it! Sponge paint dabbers or a piece of foam sponge are useful for applying both paint and glue to the inside of a vase where a brush would be awkward. Glass bowls are not a particularly good choice for decorating in this way as the inside is wholly on view and it is difficult to disguise the outline of the paper decoration, which makes it look rather odd. Unfortunately, the one drawback to applying decoration to the inside of a vase or bowl is that it cannot then be used to hold liquid (or fresh flowers) without spoiling the découpage. If you intend your project to hold liquids, you must decorate it on the outside alone, in which case you simply prepare the glass with a suitable primer and découpage it in the usual way.

Glass plates are not only the easiest, but also the most practical items to decorate beneath and, when completed, they can be used in the same way as any other plate. It is a good idea to confine your découpage decoration to the edges of plates intended for use, so that all your hard work isn't obliterated.

The craquelure technique has been applied to the glass plate before beginning the découpage process (below).

during use. To wash a decorated plate after use, simply rinse with detergent and water and dry immediately. I don't imagine anyone who has spent hours decorating a plate would even contemplate putting it in a dishwasher, but make sure you tell the rest of your household not to do so!

If you have never attempted to work on glass before, it is best to stick to a simple design using a single motif (see the celestial plate on page 57) or several unconnected motifs (see the pansy vase on page 88) to build up your confidence. Overlapping designs, such as the pansy plate below, are really the next step, but the instructions for the pansy plate apply in principle to all découpage under glass.

The découpaged pansy glass plate (below).

Pansy Glass Plate

The pretty pansies used for this plate are taken from a sheet of wrapping paper which had an overlapping design, which meant that many of the flowers were incomplete and unusable as single motifs. By arranging the design as I have, this shortcoming is disguised, although the first flower glued in place must be complete, as it is not overlapped.

The arrangement of pansies is repeated on both sides of the plate, enabling you to refer to the first half while working on the second. This method is particularly useful when working on a complicated design, such as the plate decorated with fruit on page 76.

Before beginning, make sure the glass is clean and grease-free by

washing the plate thoroughly with detergent and warm water. Leave it to drain, then polish with a lint-free cotton cloth.

YOU WILL NEED

Plain glass plate

Pansy cutouts

Latex or acrylic paint in colour of your choice

Satin water-based varnish

Clear shellac

White glue

Water-soluble marker or chinagraph pencil

Cutting mat or ruler

Low-tack adhesive spray or stick

Brushes for painting, gluing and varnishing

Damp sponge

Paper towels for applying shellac

Divide the plate into equal sections by marking the edge with a water-soluble marker or chinagraph pencil. This is easily done by placing the plate face down on a grid-marked cutting mat (**1**). Alternatively, mark the centre of the plate with a dot and use the ruler and marker to divide the plate into segments, rather like a halved orange.

Roughly cut the pansies you require from the sheet of giftwrap. Seal the back of the paper cutouts with clear shellac and, when this is dry, carefully cut out the flowers and arrange them on top of one half of the plate. Use a low-tack adhesive stick or spray that allows repositioning to hold the design in place. Repeat this layout on the other half of the plate, using the marked divisions to help with placement (**2**). If preferred, draw the outline of this arrangement on to the glass with a marker or chinagraph pencil, but take care not to go too close to the flowers or you will mark the edges of the paper.

Remove one complete pansy from the top of the plate, brush the back of the plate with a generous coating of glue to cover an area slightly larger than the pansy (3), then place the printed side of the paper in position on the back of the plate.

Press a damp sponge to the back of the glued paper, to mop up any excess glue (4), and gently ease out the tiny bubbles of air from the centre of the paper towards the edges. It is important that the sponge is not too wet as it might then damage or tear the cutout. At this stage, the paper is very slippery so you need to be careful to maintain the correct positioning. You could

use the back of your thumbnail to ease out any remaining bubbles of air, taking care not to remove too much of the glue, as that would give a patchy effect when dry. Using a clean, damp sponge, gently wipe away any excess glue (though not necessarily every trace), and continue with the next pansy until you have completed the circle.

Leave the plate to dry overnight, then check that all the edges are well stuck down. Clean off all the remaining excess glue with a damp sponge. It is safe to apply a little more pressure once the glue is dry. Any stubborn remaining glue can be removed with mineral spirits or even a scalpel, but go carefully or you may scratch the glass. Seal the back of the plate with a coat of satin water-based varnish (5) and leave to dry for two hours. This

varnish seal ensures that no paint creeps underneath the paper cutouts as there is no way to correct this mistake.

Paint the back of the plate with two coats of latex or acrylic paint (6), leaving the first to dry before applying the second. Finally, apply three coats of water-based varnish over the paint to protect the découpage during use.

1

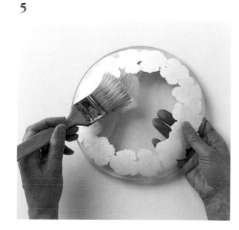

2

3

4

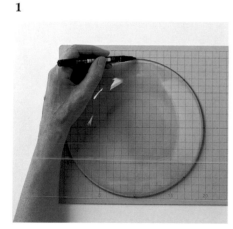

5

6

Chapter 1

CLASSICAL THEMES

*E*legant classical prints and borders
have been used in this section to give the projects a
timeless appeal. They are very easy to find
and many can be completed simply by using black-
and-white photocopies.

CLASSICAL DANCERS

A black and gold background provides a very elegant foil to the dancing ladies, while the golden craquelure adds an unusual finishing touch. Both of these accessories are made of thin metal, which enhances the delicacy of the figures.

I cut the figures out from a set of prints sold for framing. As these were already on a black background, there was no need to cut out all the enclosed areas, like those in the cherub's musical instrument on the tray. When placed over a black painted surface they become indistinguishable from it.

The tray has an unusual shape and I felt it needed some form of decoration at each end so I added a painted bow. I traced the design from a book of rococo ornaments, adapted it slightly and transferred it on to the tray.

How to achieve the look

Paint the items with black paint then decorate, following the basic découpage techniques (see page 19). Place a traced bow design in position on the tray and slide a piece of

Painting the transferred bow design.

coloured transfer paper beneath it. Trace over the design with a pencil. Fill in the transferred design with gold acrylic paint using a very fine artist's brush. Add shading to the bow with diluted black acrylic paint brushed on to the areas where the ribbon would normally fold.

Rub gilt cream on to the top and bottom rims of the wastepaper bin with your finger. Follow the basic crackle technique for the tray, rubbing gold oil paint, instead of raw umber, into the cracks. I added a drop of drying agent (Cobalt drier or Japan drier, available from art shops) to mine as the paint was bound with very slow-drying safflower oil; this speeds up the drying time.

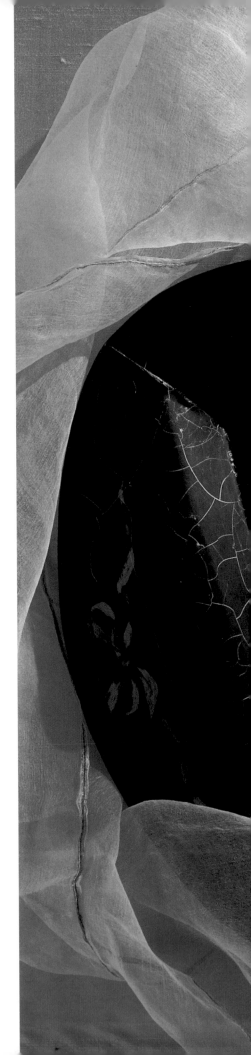

PRINT ROOM BORDERS

During the eighteenth century, a popular decorating style was to paste paper prints directly on to walls and then surround them with borders, paper ropes, garlands and other ornamental pieces. Sometimes all the walls of a room would be covered in this way. Such rooms became known as print rooms and many fine examples still exist today. Reproductions of these original borders and swags can be easily obtained (see addresses on page 142) and they adapt very well to decorating three-dimensional surfaces. They are all printed on to shades of cream-coloured paper.

The shapes of the tray, planter and umbrella stand in particular lent themselves to découpaged print room decoration. The letter rack was a little more tricky as the borders had to be made to fit the curves. The items were first painted; I used the National Trust range of latex paint colours for the base colour, and then used glazes tinted with natural earth pigments over the top.

How to achieve the look

Choose paint and glaze colours that are similarly toned for a subtle effect. I used a mix of yellow ochre and raw umber over Sudbury yellow, burnt sienna over wet sand, and venetian red over ointment pink. Make the glaze by mixing acrylic paint with acrylic gel medium and apply using either the stippling or dragging techniques described on page 22. Seal with varnish before starting.

Choose a motif for the front of the letter rack and photocopy this on cream paper to match the print room sheets. Tint all the paper with a light wash of tea to give a slightly mottled effect, before cutting out. Centre each border section and mitre the corners for a neat finish. Mitre and curve the straight borders as described on page 16, then follow the basic découpage techniques to complete.

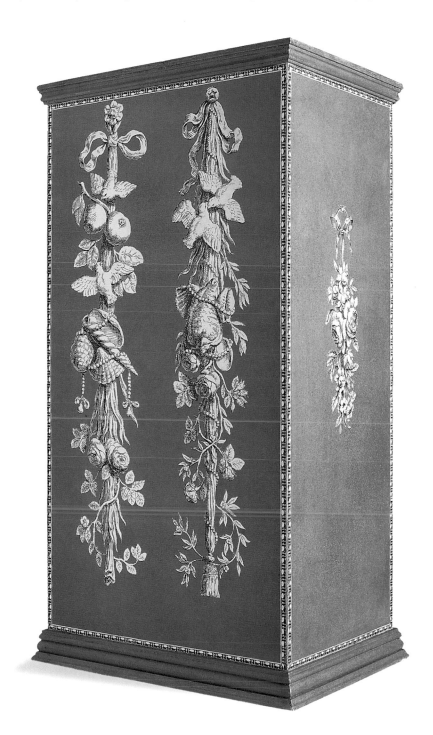

HISTORICAL ORNAMENT

There are many wonderful copyright-free books of historical ornamental designs that you can photocopy from. These include architectural ornament, book and fabric designs, as well as frames, borders and scrolls. I have used Brunelleschi architectural rosettes for the frame and nineteenth-century sculptures for the candle shades. The surrounds for the busts are from a book on frames and borders. Be creative and have fun experimenting with unusual combinations.

You will find a wide variety of candle shades and sticks readily available. The candle shades I used are actually metal, and the candlesticks are a combination of wood and metal.

The metal part of the sticks had previously been given a verdigris treatment, which didn't really suit the project I was planning. So I polished them with stove black rather than

painting over the top, to retain their metallic appearance. The plain fibreboard frame needed no preparation other than a rub down with sandpaper and a coat of paint.

How to achieve the look

Photocopy the designs on to cream-coloured paper. Enlarge and reduce the photocopies as necessary to fit the projects.

Paint the candle shades and bases the same colour. Paint a darker tone of the same colour on to each base, one at a time, and immediately dab a dishcloth over the wet paint to texture the surface.

Glue the bust on to the shade, then position the cutout frame over it, so that the base of the figure is hidden beneath the frame.

Paint the picture frame a shade of cream to match the colour of the photocopy paper. Leave to dry.

Cut some of the rosettes out completely and include a square of the background with others. This adds interest to the frame design.

Follow the basic découpage techniques (see page 19) to complete the projects.

CHERUBS

Cherubs are one of the most popular subjects for découpage. Their image appeals just as much today as it did to eighteenth-century découpeurs. There are some lovely easy-to-cut cherubs to be found in copyright-free books, but these have appeared so often that I thought I would ring the changes. Both the projects shown here feature designs that were impossible to cut out, and two ways of creating transparent images have been used to overcome this problem.

The cherub and cornucopia design on the key cupboard was copied on to white paper. A second copy was made reversing the image. If your copier is unable to do this, make an acetate copy, turn it over and copy the reverse side. Both these copies and a copy of the floral ornament on the cupboard head were turned into decals (see page 26).

The cherubs on the candle sconce were copied on to acetate and aluminum leaf was applied to the back of the copy. The leaf shines through the acetate to reflect the candlelight. The sconce was made from new galvanized steel; the stove black used to colour it has a lovely metallic quality that goes well with the black and silver design.

How to achieve the look

KEY CUPBOARD

Paint the key cupboard with off-white satin latex paint or matt paint sealed with varnish.

Make decals of the photocopies, following the instructions on page 26. Either leave a sufficient margin round the design so that you can trim it to fit the panel, or do as I did and cut round the edges of the design. This enabled me to leave out elements I did not want to use or that did not fit the shape of the panel. Glue the designs in place with transfer varnish, then apply six or more coats of varnish to the panel to disguise the edges of the cutouts.

Stipple the panel and drag the cupboard surrounds using paynes grey acrylic paint mixed with acrylic gel, following the instructions on page 22. Work in stages, in the direction of the wood grain, letting one area of wet glaze dry before applying another adjacent to it. Use masking tape to define the sections and protect the adjoining surface.

CANDLE SCONCE

Paint the sconce with black paint, as stove black will not adhere to shiny metal. Apply stove black to the sconce with a brush, leaving out the centre panel and, when dry, buff it with a soft cloth.

Photocopy the cherub design on to acetate and gild the back of it with aluminum leaf as described on page 28. Trim the design so that it fits the sconce panel exactly. Spread white glue over the panel and immediately press the photocopy firmly in place, smoothing out air bubbles. The project does not need varnishing.

Chapter 2

VICTORIAN SCRAPS

$\mathcal{V}$ictorian scraps have an enduring and nostalgic
appeal that is shared by many all over the
world. When combined with such shades of paint as
dark green or burgundy, projects can have
a strongly Victorian appearance. However, as you will
see, they do not have to be used in this way.

PAST TIMES

*I*t was a popular Victorian pastime to decorate panelled screens so that they were almost completely covered with scraps. A large central motif was often the starting point, with cutouts of various sizes added over a period of time. These larger scraps are no longer available, and decorating a large screen using only the smaller motifs would not only be very laborious, but the result would look too busy to be as effective. A firescreen is a more manageable project and you can plan the decoration from the outset to achieve a less haphazard effect than the Victorians usually did. The little boxes are more simply decorated and are ideal for beginners.

The screen here has been given an authentic Victorian look and aged with dark shellac to resemble work of that time. This project required more cutting out and arranging than any other in this book, and took several days to complete. If this is rather more time than you can commit, you could use this technique to decorate a smaller surface such as a book cover or box file. The little decorative boxes shown below are at the other end of the scale completely and these make a very good project for a beginner.

How to achieve the look

FIRESCREEN

Select sheets of scraps that don't look too incongruous together. The screen here features scraps of women, children, cherubs, and flowers, together with feathers, fans and musical instruments with pretty floral and ribbon decorations. These combine well to give cohesion to the design while the surrounding floral border pulls it all together and finishes the edges neatly.

Start by painting the background of the screen with dark green latex. A dark paint is best for this technique as it makes any gaps between the motifs less noticeable. Cut out floral border scraps to fit around the edges of the screen and glue them in place. The sections at the top of the screen will need to be cut into smaller pieces to fit round the curve. Then cut out enough scraps to cover the rest of the surface.

Begin to arrange your design roughly within the borders, starting from the top of the screen and working down, overlapping the scraps as you go. Aim for a balance of size, tone and subject. It is easier if you concentrate on the non-floral scraps first, then use flowers to fill in the gaps. Add weight to the bottom of the design by putting the light-coloured figures at the top of the screen and the darkest at the base.

In order to glue the design accurately, you will need to stick the scraps in place temporarily. Starting at the top, remove a few motifs at a time, apply repositional adhesive on the back of each cutout and press it back in position. You will probably find that you want to rearrange some scraps as you go.

When you are completely happy with the arrangement, glue the cutouts firmly into place and seal with several coats of varnish. The final yellowing of the scraps has been achieved by brushing on two coats of dark shellac.

LITTLE BOXES

These were painted in fairly strong shades of purple and yellow to reflect the colour of the pansies. Narrow floral borders were added to provide interest at the top and bottom of the sides. Follow the instructions for the basic découpage techniques (see page 19).

BEDROOM STRIPES

was recently asked to look through the archives of the Mamelok Press, who are manufacturers of Victorian scraps, and to suggest some designs that would be good to reproduce for découpage use. I immediately seized upon a pretty sheet of poppies and begged to be allowed to photocopy it for this book.

I chose this design, which is now available as a sheet of scraps, partly because the soft colouring made it so untypical and also because the ivy is very useful for linking motifs and giving flow to a design. The stripes make an unusual but effective background that sits well alongside today's home furnishings. The stripes need to be very pale so as not to overpower the delicately shaded floral cutouts. The tissue box and hat box are made from papier mâché, while the frame is fibreboard. Similar items can be found in craft shops. The stripes have been applied with a small paint roller; if you have a roller that is the width of the stripes you could dispense with the tape altogether.

How to achieve the look

Paint your projects with two coats of off-white paint, allowing the first coat to dry before applying the second. It is preferable to apply this with a paint roller so that the background surface has the same texture as the stripes.

When the paint is dry, measure the circumference of the base of the hat box with a tape measure. Divide this figure into an even number of stripes of equal width. Using a tape measure and pencil, mark the position of the stripes around the box sides. Stick masking tape in place on the outside edge of alternate marks, checking to see that each line is vertical. Mark a stripe the same width as used for the base across the centre of the lid. Mark further stripes on each side of this and mask these in the same way.

The tissue box is easier to mark as each section of the box is simply divided into two stripes. Mark the base so that the coloured stripes are opposite to those on the lid.

Paint all the stripes with two coats of pale green paint, using a paint roller. Then paint the top of the tissue box and the edge of the frame with green paint. Remove the tape and follow the basic découpage techniques for applying the designs (see page 19).

Apply paint over the tape strips.

ANTIQUE EFFECTS

The ancient-looking rooster cupboard would be very appropriate for a country kitchen. The chicken wire has been faked by clever use of the photocopier and a sheet of acetate, which has the added benefit of replacing layers of varnish. The rooster was copied from a book of copyright-free scraps and has been enlarged to fit the panel. The sludgy purple border and yellowing crackled surface of the fruity tray give it a more Victorian appearance.

How to achieve the look

ROOSTER CUPBOARD

Photocopy a piece of chicken wire on to white paper, then copy this on to a sheet of acetate. Copying directly on to acetate can leave a shadow. Paint the centre panel of the wooden cupboard with cream paint and leave to dry. Trim the acetate chicken wire to fit this exactly. Paint the cupboard surrounds with a terracotta shade to highlight the rooster, protecting the paint on the panel with masking tape.

Follow the wax resist distressed paint effect (see page 22) for applying the second colour.

Glue the rooster in position and leave to dry. Spread white glue over the panel and place the acetate on top. Press the acetate down very firmly to eliminate any air bubbles towards the edges of the panel. When dry, varnish the outside of the cupboard with two coats of matt varnish, then apply brown wax over the top.

FRUIT TRAY

Paint a small wooden tray with cream paint. Allow to dry, then add a purple border to the rim using a single layer of paint. When this is dry, rub fine-grade sandpaper over the surface so that some of the cream paint shows through the purple. Follow the instructions for the basic découpage and craquelure techniques (see pages 19 and 31) to decorate and complete the tray.

Chapter 3

Contemporary Ideas

*S*tunning contemporary giftwraps, gilded suns, self-
adhesive stars, brightly coloured watercolour inks,
gingham and handmade paper are all used to create
an exciting range of innovative designs.

CELESTIAL DREAMS

When I came across Patrick Mauriès book on Piero Fornasetti, Fornasetti: Designer of Dreams, I could not believe my good fortune. Almost every page provided inspirational designs, many of which could translate into découpage. Here was a masterly use of two-dimensional printed images to decorate three-dimensional designs and I could only wonder that, to my knowledge, nobody else had already made this connection. One particularly striking image was of a malachite dish decorated with gold musical instruments and I set to thinking about how I might create similar golden images. The answer lay in photocopying black-and-white designs on to acetate, and then applying gold leaf to these transparent images before cutting them out. The results that can be achieved with this process are simply stunning.

A sun with a face, in particular a woman's face, is a recurring image in Fornasetti's designs; he was certainly a designer with a sense of humour and style. To produce the designs shown in the photographs on these pages, I have drawn from several of Fornasetti's ideas and put them to practical use to give a completely new look to the craft of découpage. The unusual and beautiful galvanized steel items used

in this section certainly play a part in this new look and give an extra dimension which would be absent from plainer, more solidly built pieces of furniture.

The clever design of the table top resembles a cloth and I have added to this textile illusion by draping images over the sides of the table. Go ahead, experiment and have fun with your découpage – I certainly have with these beautiful images!

How to achieve the look

Paint all the items that are to be découpaged, apart from the glass plate, with black paint.

Find appropriate celestial images in books of copyright-free designs and use them as they are, or design your own versions as follows. Copy different faces and sunbursts, enlarging and reducing them in size. Then cut out the faces and lay them over the various sunbursts to create new images. Photocopy your chosen designs on to acetate.

Carefully brush a layer of acrylic gold size on to the side of the acetate that is inked.

Leave the gold size to dry for fifteen minutes or more if possible, then carefully lay the sized surface of the acetate over a sheet of metal leaf. Separate the backing from the acetate and cut out the design.

Glue the acetate images to the surface with white glue. This will take some time to dry, perhaps even several days for large motifs. Where a cutout folds over an edge, hold it firmly in place with a strip or two of masking tape until it is completely dry. Check that all the edges are well stuck down and re-glue any that are not. You may need to be fairly persistent with the folded motifs, but

those that lie flat are not usually a problem. When the design is thoroughly dry, apply three or more coats of satin acrylic varnish, allowing each coat to dry before applying the next.

To provide a contrast, the plate has been gilded and decorated with black-and-white paper images. The legs of the table have also been gilded, leaving gaps to reveal small blotches of black paint here and there. Do not varnish the gilded surfaces as they would then lose their lustre. If you need to protect the legs from damage, brush them with a coat of clear shellac.

MONOCHROME MOTIFS

*B*lack-and-white photocopies on a white background provide a strong visual impact and allow the paper to blend almost imperceptibly with the paint. I had a great deal of fun with the umbrella stand, assembling motifs from five different sources and playing around with scale until I achieved the design I had in mind. The architectural, sun and cloud motifs were Fornasetti-inspired, while the hot-air balloon was an added touch of mine. For style on a shoestring, you can transform cheap glass plates and a plain white ceramic vase with monochrome motifs.

The most difficult problem I had when designing the umbrella stand was finding the clouds. There always seemed to be trees, buildings or cherubs in the way. In the end I took small sections of cloud and enlarged them greatly, hence the slightly odd shapes! The star motif vase is instant découpage, as it is like decorating with stickers. It is not intended to be permanent and you can give it a make-over when it starts to look tired.

How to achieve the look

Paint the exterior of the umbrella stand white and the inside, top and bottom rims black. Follow the instructions on page 23 for painting curved borders and complete the project using the basic découpage techniques (see page 19).

To create a sun plate, follow the découpage under glass technique on page 34. You will need to use at least three coats of white latex paint.

For the ceramic vase, photocopy black-and-white star motifs on to self-adhesive acetate. Seal the photocopy ink with clear shellac before cutting the stars out. Separate the acetate from the backing sheet and press the cutout directly on to the ceramic surface. Do not varnish.

BRIGHT GINGHAMS

S̲trong colours and simple shapes look stunning on a gingham background and this painted technique is very simple to do. The flowers, fruit and vegetables were cut from contemporary giftwrap, which was designed using historical sources. A similar look can be achieved by colouring black-and-white photocopies with bright paints. The storage jars were painted with ceramic paints directly over the glazed surface, while the flower pots were painted with white latex paint before being decorated with bright acrylic colours.

There are several paints on the market that are suitable for ceramic surfaces. The type I used were water-based and required baking in a domestic oven at a low temperature. I was surprised at how successful they proved, with the paint staying firmly in place even when the masking tape was removed from the surface.

Rather than placing two strips of tape to create a line for painting, the tape was used merely to define the width of stripes. It is removed before painting, so that the effect looks more hand-painted. The cutout motifs rather than the jar surface were varnished. This means that the jars retain their glossy appearance, and can be wiped clean.

How to achieve the look

STORAGE JARS

Stick vertical strips of low-tack 1.25cm (¹/₂ in) masking tape all around the jar. You can usually space them fairly evenly by eye if you put the second strip on the other side of the jar, opposite the first, and then

the third and fourth strips half way between these two and so on. Draw a line down either side of each strip of masking tape, then remove it. Place horizontal bands around the jars and proceed in the same way to complete the gingham effect. Fill in the marked areas with ceramic paint using a soft

synthetic brush and cure in the oven according to the manufacturer's instructions.

Cut out the motifs and seal with either two coats of spray varnish or white glue. Stick the designs on to the jars with white glue.

Draw a line on each side of the tape.

Apply paint within the marked bands.

FLOWER POTS

Paint the flower pots with two coats of white latex paint. Leave to dry. Mask and mark the flower pots to create the gingham effect, in the same way as for the jars. Use acrylic paint mixed with acrylic gel medium to paint the stripes.

Complete the decoration of the flower pots following the basic découpage technique (see page 19).

Fine Feathers

I really like feathers but cannot explain why they have the same kind of appeal for me as do shells. Perhaps it is because they share a natural pattern-making quality. Shells would work equally well on all of these projects. Beautiful handmade papers using organic and recycled materials, together with unpainted wood, are a pleasing combination that fits well with the natural decorating style that is currently so popular.

The paper shade, frame and box were all chain store buys, and it is quite easy to find similar plain varnished wooden pieces you can decorate. You will find handmade papers in your local art shop or specialist paper supplier. I matched the handmade paper on the frame and box as closely as I could to the ready-made shade.

How to achieve the look

Look out for feathered giftwrap or other natural-coloured motifs, such as shells. Cut squares or strips of paper, wiggling the scissors as you go, so the edges resemble those that you find on handmade papers.

Glue the paper in position on the project surfaces. This type of paper is usually very soft and absorbent, and it tends to bubble and stretch. However, as long as you make sure that you have smoothed out all air bubbles towards the edges of the paper, you will find that it shrinks back and becomes smooth as it dries. You might find it helpful to use a lino printing roller to flatten the paper and smooth out bubbles.

Follow the instructions for basic découpage techniques (see page 19) for the shade and the wooden items. The gluing process will probably make the handmade paper wrinkle, as will wetting with varnish, but it will shrink back into place.

Varnish the items with two or three coats of matt varnish. A shiny appearance spoils the effect and you will lose the lovely textural quality of the shade and paper if you cover it with too many layers of varnish.

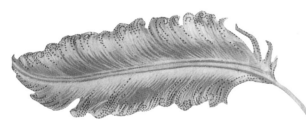

SIMPLE HEARTS

If you really want to impress, present a gift in a découpaged box or one of these papier mâché bags. The simple cutting out and easy gilding are quickly done and this is not the labour of love that it appears. The cutouts on the trash can will appeal to teenage daughters, although you might find they want to have their own say in the design.

The quality of design on some ranges of contemporary giftwrap is outstanding. The papers used for these projects, and for those on the next four pages, have all been produced by the same manufacturer. With their easy-to-cut shapes, they lend themselves well to découpage. You will find the supplier's address at the back of the book.

If you are not able to find similar bags, use a cardboard box instead.

How to achieve the look

WASTEPAPER CAN

Paint the can with latex paint and leave to dry. Apply a second colour over this using a sponge, so that most of the first coat is covered and only a touch of the base colour shows through. Two shades of purple latex paint were used for this bin; the lighter shade was sponged over the darker one. Complete the project using the basic découpage techniques (see page 19).

GILDED BAGS

Paint your project with a primary-coloured paint. When dry, stick a narrow strip of masking tape around the edges to form a border and apply metal leaf on to the surface, following the basic gilding technique on page 28. Follow the basic découpage techniques (see page 19), but replace the paste glue with white glue as it is better for sticking paper to metal leaf. Three coats of varnish are adequate for this project. It is best to use satin varnish as matt varnish makes the metal leaf look dull.

HARVEST TIME

Although these garden carriers have been hand-crafted to traditional country designs, they have been decorated with modern giftwraps and fresh coloured washes of paint, which give a contemporary feel. The trailing peel of the orange and lemon lend a nice informality to the carrier design and provide a contrast to the more formal fruit arrangements in the next chapter. If you prefer a more traditional approach, you could use old seed packets or cuttings from garden catalogues and tone down the colouring.

I have a penchant for lime green at the moment and decided on this colouring for these garden carriers. I used thin washes of colour to allow the projects to keep their wood-like appearance. When I started to arrange the designs in place, the fruit designs looked reasonably good, but the darker vegetables and flower pots did not. The answer seemed to lie in adding darker streaks of colour to tone down the effect. Using thin washes of colour allows you to alter the colour as you go, lightening or darkening as appropriate.

How to achieve the look

Paint the wood with a coat of white latex paint, diluted with approximately 10 parts water to 1 part paint. This will give you a light base to start with. Brush on a thinned coat of lime green paint. Wipe over the wet surface with a dishcloth to remove some of the paint. Repeat this process if you wish. Then brush diluted dark green paint over this in streaky patches and leave to dry. Finally, brush a thinned coat of white latex paint over the top. When dry, rub off some of the paint in places with fine sandpaper.

Follow the basic découpage techniques (see page 19) to complete the projects, then finish with two coats of matt acrylic varnish.

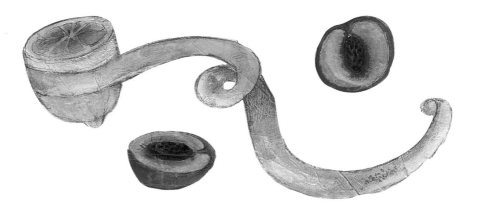

HOME SWEET HOME

*D*ecorating a project with motifs that relate to its intended use is always appropriate, and I was delighted to find such pretty and unusual designs on contemporary giftwrap. I felt the background colour for the projects needed to reflect the loose and painterly quality of the motifs and I rubbed thin washes of diluted latex over the base paint to achieve the subtle textured effect. The tray was a very cheap tin one decorated with a horrible pattern – you probably know the sort. If you have one of these, now is your chance to make it beautiful.

How to achieve the look

SEWING BOX

Paint the box with pale blue paint. Brush a very thin coat of bright blue over this, and dab it with a dishcloth to blend it into the surface. Apply a final wash of thinned white latex paint. Arrange the motifs on the box and proceed with the basic découpage techniques (see page 19).

TRAY

Paint the tray with off-white or white with a hint of pink. Make two different colours of pink-red washes, picking out shades that appear on the motifs. Brush each colour on in turn, blending the paint with a dishcloth and working quickly. Repeat these two colours, then brush over a wash

of diluted off-white or pink-white. Use a more concentrated mix of the same two colours to paint the darker border, then finish this with the off-white wash. Complete the tray using the basic découpage techniques (see page 19). You will need to pay particular attention to the spaces between motifs when using irregular shapes like this.

COLOUR CONTRASTS

These colourful motifs began as plain black-and-white photocopies of historical engravings, which were then coloured with watercolour inks. The off-white paint on the backgrounds is used to emphasize the strong shapes and colours and the boldly-painted borders complete the look. The square pots would look lovely filled with leafy green plants, but you should put a saucer inside a wooden box, and should only put soil directly into ceramic pots if they are glazed on the inside, otherwise water will seep through and damage the découpaged surface.

The square box was finished with a look of peeling paint, with liming wax rubbed into the cracked surface. A water-based crackle glaze is sandwiched between two layers of paint to achieve this effect. It is essential that you use a fairly thin latex paint that flows easily from the brush, as the paint is effectively laid over the glaze, rather than brushed on. A soft, flat varnish brush is best used for this.

How to achieve the look

PLANTERS

Paint all the projects with off-white paint. Paint contrasting borders in bright colours, using masking tape to protect the base colour. Paint the inside of the pots with a contrasting colour if appropriate. Colour the photocopies following the instructions on page 27 and continue with the basic découpage techniques (see page 19).

SQUARE BOX

Paint the lid of the box off-white. Create a border around the edge of the lid with masking tape. Paint this border and the remainder of the box bright blue. Remove the masking tape, then continue with the basic découpage techniques (see page 19).

Place strips of masking tape on the inside edge of the découpaged square to protect the surface. Brush water-based crackle glaze on to the lid edge and the remaining blue surface. Leave to dry overnight. Apply a second coat of blue paint over this, taking care not to go over an area just painted, or you will reactivate the glaze and the paint will start to slide. When dry, fill in any bits you might have missed with a small brush. Rub liming wax into the surface with 00-grade steel wool. Leave for half an hour, then remove the excess wax from the surface with steel wool and clear wax. Buff to shine and remove the masking tape. This surface is not suitable for applying découpage.

Chapter 4

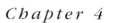

FRUITS
OF THE EARTH

If you are wondering how to decorate items for the kitchen and dining room, then fruit could be the elegant and mouthwatering answer.

FRUITS AND FUNGI

I found these lovely fruit and fungi motifs on some Italian giftwraps. The soft colours and simple shapes of the fruit make this a very versatile paper. You can arrange the fruit individually, in groups or in an overlapping arrangement as the plate on page 76 illustrates. The small motifs adapt easily to being used on a variety of different-shaped surfaces and provided the perfect answer for these prettily-shaped dishes. The toadstool paper is so unusual that it seems quite odd to use it for wrapping a gift, but it is wonderful for découpage.

Unlike the fruit, the toadstools were already grouped together in threes and fours. The red toadstools in the centre of the design were not quite as bright as I wanted, so I cheated a little and enhanced the red by painting a little watercolour paint on with an artist's brush. The inside of

the galvanized steel planter has been brushed with a bright chalky red paint and it looks as if I have been very clever with a paint finish. In fact I haven't – the lovely textural quality of the paint surface is merely a reaction between the paint and the primed metal surface.

How to achieve the look

Paint the fruit dishes with soft paint colours and the planter an off-white. Paint the inside of the planter red to match the colour of the toadstools.

Then follow the instructions for basic découpage and antiquing on pages 19 and 30. Experiment with different fruit arrangements until you find a

design you are happy with. Finish with a coat of matt varnish then apply brown wax over this to complete the antiqued look.

SUMMER FRUITS

This beautiful glass plate is by far the most difficult project in the book, but I felt it was worth the effort and this is one of the few pieces I have ever made that I intend to keep. The difficult part of this project was gluing the overlapping design in place in the reverse order, beneath the glass. The small cherries and berry fruits had to be stuck down first, instead of on top of the large fruits, as would be the case if the arrangement was on top of the plate. Careful marking was required to make sure that the two halves of the plate had a symmetrical arrangement. This is not a project for the impatient!

This plate is very large, nearly 38cm (15in) in diameter. It actually had a gold rim when I purchased it, but you could add your own to the back of the plate, by gilding a border before you start the decoration. Once the découpaged design was sealed in place, the plate was sponged with a subtle ageing paint glaze, to add a touch of colour and give a soft mottled look to the background of the plate.

How to achieve the look

Divide the plate into eight segments, rather like an orange. Mark the segments on top of the plate with a marker pen.

Seal the back of the paper you are using, rather than the printed surface, with clear shellac. Cut out the fruit motifs and arrange them on the top of one half of the plate within four segments. Use a repositional spray adhesive underneath the cutouts to keep them in place while you do this.

Complete an identical arrangement on the underside of the opposite half of the plate. Look at the arrangement on top to see where each motif is placed within a segment and use repositional glue on the front of the motifs to hold in place. Next, transfer the prints that you have arranged on top to the underside. This is easier if you just remove a few at a time. These will need temporary glue on the printed surface to hold them in place and this glue will now be on both sides of the print. Apart from being rather sticky to handle, this

doesn't seem to matter and sticky residue can easily be removed afterwards with lighter fuel or mineral spirit and a soft cloth.

You should now have a completed design underneath the plate ready for gluing permanently in place. This

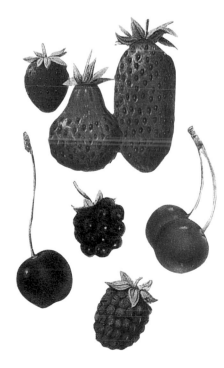

means that you will have to remove at least two or three motifs in order to do this. To make it easier, draw lines around the shapes of the designs on top of the plate. You needn't draw them all, you need just enough to mark the position. Then glue the designs accurately in place and remove the marks. Refer to the découpage under glass section (see page 34) to complete the gluing and sealing processes.

Mix together some raw umber and yellow ochre acrylic paint, then add some acrylic gel medium and a little water to this so that you have a dirty yellow glaze. Dab this lightly over the varnished surface with a natural sea sponge. It is quite hard to see the effect unless you hold it over a white or pale surface.

Leave the glaze to dry for several hours, then paint the back of the plate with three coats of off-white paint, followed by two or three coats of acrylic varnish. Now stand back and admire your work!

TRAILING VINES

These grapes formed part of a Florentine pietre dure *border design, which I found reproduced on wrapping paper. The rather angular shape of the grapes is not due to poor cutting-out, I might add, but to the fact that, incredibly, the design has been crafted in stone. The intricate cutting-out involved in creating these projects hardly bears mention when you think of the painstaking work of producing the original. I used the design untypically to decorate country items, but you will see the same paper used on pages 132–3 in a way that is more akin to the original style.*

A matching tray and wine carrier make a good project for a kitchen or dining room. Similar trays are easily found, and the wine carrier can be obtained from the address at the back of the book. Although the items I have used have a very wooden appearance, the base of the tray is actually made of white board and not wood at all. After sanding and priming this surface with a suitable primer, I painted the background colour with straight brush strokes across the width of the wood in the direction the grain would normally be. The glaze is caught in these brush marks and gives the impression of being wood. The background has been painted with a cool, neutral off-white and a paynes grey glaze has been softly dragged over this with a cloth. This glaze effectively adds a grey dirt instead of the brown raw umber dirt that I normally use, giving a stone-like quality to the pieces.

How to achieve the look

Look for suitable fruity cutouts to decorate a matching tray and wine carrier. Paint the projects with off-white paint. Mix together paynes grey acrylic paint with acrylic gel medium and water. Paint this roughly over the surface. Make a pad with a piece of dishcloth and drag this over the wet glaze to remove most of the paint and give it a very soft, dragged look. Work on one surface at a time. It is slightly more difficult to drag inside the bottle carrier and you probably won't get such a neat effect, but this is nothing to worry about. Follow the basic découpage techniques (see page 19) to complete the projects.

BOTANICAL STUDIES

The beautifully-illustrated fruit on the square planters is the work of William Hooker and those on the tray are by Pierre-Joseph Redouté. These early nineteenth-century studies have a timeless appeal and the boldness and simplicity of design make them perfect for découpage use. You can find similar fruit illustrations on prints, postcards or in books. The unusually-shaped items are all made from unpainted galvanized steel, and are intended to be used as such. However, I can't help feeling that they would sit more comfortably in most people's homes once they have been decorated.

How to achieve the look

Choose dark traditional paint colours, such as red ochre, or murky blues and greens which look so good with the fruit. Brush the paint on in a random way, with cross-hatched brush strokes. Follow the instructions on pages 19 and 30 for the basic découpage and antiquing techniques. Use butterflies and other insects to fill any gaps in the design.

Brush a final coat or two of matt acrylic varnish over the satin varnish, allowing each coat to dry before applying another, and polish with brown wax. If you want your tray to be heatproof, replace the matt acrylic varnish with two coats of oil-based polyurethane varnish instead. If you choose a matt varnish, you can still polish the surface with wax if you like.

FLORENTINE FEASTS

These deliciously exquisite bowls of fruit were painted during the seventeenth century and not only are they perfectly proportioned to decorate these table mats, they are also very appropriate. I felt that a simple background was required so as not to detract from the beauty of the paintings, so I sponged a delicate ageing glaze over a cream background.

How to achieve the look

Decide how many mats you require and look for appropriate fruity découpage designs.

Paint the mats with off-white paint. Make a dirty-looking paint by mixing together roughly equal quantities of yellow ochre and raw umber acrylic colour with acrylic gel medium and a little water. Sponge this over each mat very sparingly, preferably using a natural sea sponge, and do not dab an area more than once or you will spoil the textured effect.

Complete the project following the basic découpage techniques (see page 19). Acrylic varnish is suitable for warm to hot plates, but if you want them to be really heatproof, you will need to apply two coats of oil-based polyurethane varnish over the acrylic. As oil varnishes tend to be yellowish, this will alter the colour of the mats a little.

PINEAPPLES

I find it hard to believe that this amazing and stylish pineapple print is from a hand-tinted etching dated 1697. I was instantly attracted to this wonderful design when I found it and wondered what on earth I could use it on. This churn proved the perfect shape, but now I'm wondering what to do with a churn. In fact, beautifully-decorated items do not need to serve a purpose. Just admire your designs and look on them as three-dimensional art.

The pineapple design may look simple and easy to cut at first glance, but if you take a closer look, you will see dozens of serrated edges on the leaves. My mother cut out this pineapple for me and it was definitely a labour of love! You may not find a design quite like this, but it is possible that you will come across other awkward and unusual shapes that need to be found a home. You might be able to reduce or enlarge the design to fit a shape, or add little motifs to fill gaps, like the winged creatures I have added to the top part of the churn.

How to achieve the look

Paint the churn a soft pale blue. Age the wooden handles by staining with a water-based walnut wood dye. Follow the instructions on pages 19 and 30 for the basic découpage and antiquing techniques. To complete, use a matt varnish for the two final coats, then polish with brown wax.

Chapter 5

FLORAL DISPLAY

*utch flowers, botanical illustrations and pretty
bouquets and motifs are all easy to find.
This is just as well, since floral papers are surely the
most popular of all for découpage.*

PRETTY PANSIES

The Victorians were very fond of decorating with pansies, and these pretty flowers are still popular today. Their wonderful colour range and distinctive flowerheads are a designer's dream. The pansy projects on both these pages have come from the same sheet of giftwrap, but they have been given a very different treatment. The metal items on the right have been given a strongly aged appearance, while the glass ones below have a fresh, bright look.

For an aged look like this, I have developed my own crackle technique, using a water-based crackle glaze beneath a clear acrylic glaze. This is much the same as the peeling paint technique used for the square box on page 71, but with a rottenstone paint worked into the cracks. You can use raw umber pigment instead, but rottenstone is softer and more neutral in colour. All these products are available from specialist paint suppliers.

How to achieve the look

CANDLE HOLDER AND PLANTER

Paint the items with soft faded paint colours that complement those of the pansies; I used an old-fashioned shade of lilac. Then follow the instructions for the basic découpage techniques (see page 19).

Brush a coat of water-based crackle glaze over the last coat of varnish, and leave to dry overnight. Lay a coat of acrylic glaze over this and allow it to dry overnight again so that the mediums become more stable. To apply the acrylic glaze, follow the instructions on page 71 for laying on paint. Take an empty yoghurt carton or similar container and half-fill it with water. Add enough rottenstone and water to make a thin, but not watery, paint and bind this with a few drops of gum arabic. Brush this on to the surface with a soft brush and leave it to dry. Then wipe the excess off the surface with a damp sponge. You need to take care not to rub the surface too hard or you may damage it. Leave to dry, then rub brown wax into the surface and polish. Alternatively, you can seal the cracks with acrylic varnish if you prefer.

This technique may take some practice, but the cracking is less regular and the results are quite different from any crackle kit on the market. If you think this sounds too complicated or you want a quicker result, replace this with the antiquing paint process on page 30.

GLASS PLATE AND VASE

Choose light but crisp, clear paint and stronger-coloured flowers. The instructions for decorating the plate are on page 34, and for the glass vase on pages 33–34. The glass vase is purely decorative and should not be used to hold water.

REDOUTÉ ROSES

P̲ierre-Joseph Redouté was probably better known for his rose paintings than for any others. These exquisite studies first appeared in a now-famous work called Les Roses, *which was published in sections between 1817 and 1824. The popularity of these paintings has ensured their reproduction on a wide range of material, from postcards and books to all sizes of prints. This range of sizes has enabled to me to decorate the 10cm (4in) high planter with the same design as the 50cm (20in) flower bucket, while the milk churn is decorated with similar roses that are a size in between.*

All the decorated items are made from galvanized steel and the large flower bucket is big enough to serve as an umbrella stand. When I sold my découpaged designs, my poor mother used to spend many hours cutting out the serrated leaf edges and thorny stems on the roses to keep me going with a regular supply of motifs! I nearly always found that my customers preferred the roses shown against a soft light background. However, they also look very striking on a dark-coloured background.

How to achieve the look

Paint all the items with soft, muted colours. To paint a contrasting rose-coloured interior to the planter, dilute a dusky rose latex paint with about 50 per cent water. Brush this on the inside surface and immediately dab over the wet paint with a dishcloth.

Follow the basic découpage techniques (see page 19) for all the projects, and the antiquing paint technique (see page 30) for the churn and flower bucket. Complete these two items with matt varnish, then polish with brown wax. Follow the craquelure technique on page 32 to complete the exterior surface of the planter.

Floral Wreath

This wreath of wild roses was painted by Redouté as a frontispiece for Les Roses, *his wonderful collection of rose paintings published in the nineteenth century. It is so unlike the formal single stems in the rest of the work and is perfect for decorating a round surface. It didn't fit quite so easily around this beautiful glass dish, because the surface was curved. The solution was to divide the cutout into sections and overlap them where necessary to fit the curve.*

The pedestal dish is similar to the glass plate featured on page 77 and has also been decorated with a circular edging design. The main difference between the two projects is that the fruit plate had a complicated arrangement of overlapping motifs, while the design of the roses is already overlapping and time is saved on arranging. The gluing process, however, was trickier. This was partly due to keeping the leaf stems and other fine parts intact and also the need to rejoin accurately the divided parts while disguising the overlap.

How to achieve the look

Seal the back of the print with clear shellac, then cut out the wreath and divide it into four sections. These will

Assembling the sections of the wreath.

not necessarily be of equal size as you will need to make a cut so that each divided area has complete petals and leaf shapes on one side. In some cases this will mean that both ends of a section have completed shapes. In others, neither will and the section will rely on the adjoining edge overlapping to disguise this fact. This is not as difficult as it might sound; it simply requires time to think it through carefully. If you wish, mark lightly with a pencil where you are going to make a division. Arrange the sections in position on the bowl and use repositional glue to hold them in place. Draw around the outline on top of the plate with a felt-tip pen.

Refer to the instructions for découpage under glass (see page 34) before commencing the gluing. You will need to stretch and ease the damp paper to fit the curved surface. Leave the incomplete end unglued and slide the completed edge in place beneath it. Where you have overlapped paper, take extra care to smooth out bubbles of air. Continue until all the sections are in place, then seal the design with acrylic varnish.

Choose a shade of green paint that suits the green leaf colouring and brush two or three coats on to the back of the plate. Finally, seal with three coats of acrylic varnish.

ENAMEL ROSES

*O*ld enamel is lovely to decorate and it doesn't much matter what condition it is in as any chips and dents just add to the aged effect. One of my students kindly presented me with this bowl, which was a perfect partner for a jug I already had and I decorated them both with romantic roses for a pretty bedroom look.

It is very easy to find old enamel in junk shops but cheaper pieces nearly always seems to have some degree of rust. This must be treated or all your hard work decorating it will be spoilt. And a word of warnng: don't buy a jug that has completely rusted through at the bottom if you want it to hold water! The flowers were cut from the wrapping paper design at the foot of the page. You will see

that you can produce a simple design by taking individual motifs from quite a complicated arrangement. I extracted the lovely generous rosy blooms from the sheet and left behind all the fiddly bits that were difficult to cut out. A certain amount of leaf rearrangement and joining together of different parts was required to balance the final découpaged design.

How to achieve the look

Paint the jug and bowl with a coat of eggshell blue paint, then refer to the basic découpage techniques (see page 19) to decorate. Cut out more flowers than you think you might need so that you can try out different designs.

Arranging the découpaged design on the bowl is simple and straightforward but you will need to experiment with different arrangements to find one that suits the shape of the jug. Use repositional glue to hold the motifs in place.

Use the antiquing paint over the second coat of varnish as described on page 30. Rub most of it off, leaving a touch of brown paint for a subtle effect. Complete the project by applying two coats of matt varnish over the last satin layer.

ORCHIDS

Sunflowers, pansies, tulips and particularly auriculas have all enjoyed enormous popularity recently, and their stylized forms have been used by many designers. For some reason, orchids have not had their share of the lime-light, so I hope I can tip the balance a little by using these nineteenth-century orchid prints which are not only unusual but also very beautiful.

How to achieve the look

Look out for books, prints and postcards of orchids. Museums and garden shops and the natural history sections of good bookshops should provide a starting point. Keep an eye out for unusually-shaped items to decorate. Apart from the flower pot, all of the items here are galvanized steel; similar ones can be found in garden and home decorating stores.

Follow the instructions for basic découpage and antiquing techniques (see pages 19 and 30). Choose soft, natural colours to balance with the subtle colouring of the plants. Use butterflies and insects to add interest to undecorated areas which may look a little bare. To finish, use a matt varnish for the two final coats, then polish with brown wax.

DUTCH FLOWERS

*V*oluptuous floral bouquets arranged masterfully in urns, baskets or vases, were painted by the great Dutch flower painters of the seventeenth and early eighteenth century and are readily available on giftwrap. These papers have been used extensively for découpaged designs and, as they have appeared in many books and magazines, I thought I would try to show them in a less familiar light by painting the projects a striking Chinese yellow, then adding a sponged texture.

It is not without reason that these Dutch flower giftwraps are so popular. The designs are not only beautiful but they can also be used successfully to decorate all shapes and sizes of projects, from a small box to a large piece of furniture. You simply need to cut out different flowerheads or sections from the giftwrap and rearrange them on a surface, overlapping the pieces as necessary. You can use more than one sheet of a design, or combine it with other sheets to complete larger-sized projects.

How to achieve the look

Paint the projects with a fairly bright yellow satin latex paint or matt latex sealed with acrylic varnish. Mix some yellow ochre acrylic paint with a little raw umber and add acrylic gel medium to the mix. A little water can be added to achieve the desired effect. Apply this colour over the yellow paint using a natural sea sponge. Dab the surface repeatedly to even out the texture. This glaze will take away a little of the brightness without killing the colour. Paint a band of the same colour, but without gel, on to the top and bottom rims of the coal scuttle.

Use the basic découpage techniques (see page 19) to complete the projects and finish with two coats of matt varnish. Take note of the additional information below for gluing the design on the firescreen.

You can divide the paper into smaller sections and reassemble them on the screen. However, thin wrapping paper tends to stretch, and if you are joining several pieces together, rather

like a jigsaw puzzle, you may find that the pieces have stretched to varying degrees and it can be tricky re-joining them accurately and invisibly.

This flower design was glued to the screen in one complete piece, which was neater, quicker and not very difficult to do. Use repositional adhesive on the back of the paper to hold the design accurately in place to start. Lift the bottom section up a few inches and brush a band of paste across the width of the screen in its place. Press the paper firmly in position, smoothing out all bubbles of air towards the paper edges, using a lino roller if possible. Then lift up the top edge of the paper, peel it back as far as the glued area and brush on another band of paste about four or five inches wide. Make sure that there are no gaps in the pasting between this and the previously glued band. Smooth down the paper and press or roll air bubbles upwards and outwards away from the previously glued area. Continue until the whole design is in place.

AURICULAS

$\mathcal{A}$ uriculas seem to be the flower of the moment; by auriculas I mean the painted versions. I have to say printed auriculas look more stunning than any real ones that I have seen, but then, to be fair, I haven't come across that many. The single auriculas were cut from thinned postcards, while those on the picnic carrier are, not for the first time in this section, Redouté prints. I make no apologies for this, as his designs lend themselves to découpage so well.

The yellow basket, with its area for holding bottles and a lidded section for food, was described as a picnic carrier by the company from which I bought it. I used to decorate these for sale and, for some of my customers, the so-called picnic carrier seems to have been a different sort of familiar shape from the past. Some said that the lidded section was for holding water and the end section was for cloths, others that one section was for polishes and the other brushes. Either way, it served a very unglamorous purpose!

How to achieve the look

You can replace the picnic carrier with a bucket, planter or other item to create a similar look. Paint your chosen project with a golden yellow ochre to match the yellow on the auriculas. Paint the flower pots and wine holder using subtle colours that harmonize with those of the auriculas. Follow the basic découpage and antiquing paint techniques (see pages 19 and 30) for all the projects, using a matt varnish to finish. Rub gilt cream with your finger on to the top and bottom rims of the wine holder. Finally, bring out the richness of colour on the picnic carrier by applying a yellowing antique pine wax.

COTTAGE GARDEN

I enjoy decorating items for a conservatory or garden room where floral designs are very appropriate. The unusual colouring and leaf shape of these tulips particularly attracted me, and the Victorian pansy bouquet is simply so pretty. The choice of print was the starting point in both these cases and selecting an item to decorate with them came second. The tall plain jug suited the tulips well while the pansies fit perfectly on the pretty scallop-edged planter. I took the opposite approach with the hanging plant holder, which is ideal for a conservatory wall, simply decorating it with a favourite flower that fit the available surface area.

How to achieve the look

Gather together a few galvanized steel items suitable for containing plants or flowers and match them with appropriate prints. Some items can be obtained from the supplier listed at the back of the book (see page 143).

Paint the jug and planter with a coat of off-white paint and the hanging planter with a coat of soft green. Use a traditional chalky paint if you want to achieve the mottled paint effect that results from the reaction between the primed metal surface and the paint. Leave to dry thoroughly before applying the découpaged decoration. If you do not want to use the jug for holding fresh flowers, paint the inside with a purple-brown shade of paint to match the tulip colouring; otherwise, simply leave it unpainted.

Complete the projects by following the basic découpage techniques on page 19. Allow to dry thoroughly, then use the antiquing paint after the second coat of varnish as described on page 30. Apply a final coat of matt varnish over the satin varnish and polish with brown wax to add to the antiqued effect.

FLORA AND FAUNA

*T*he delicately-woven wreath of leaves, butterflies and moths is a hand-coloured engraving for a decorative title page from an eighteenth-century natural history book. I think this design gave elegance to a rather solid and plain-looking metal sconce. The winged insects on the flower pots are taken from eighteenth- and nineteenth-century sources, and the dragonfly formed part of a lithograph called *Insect Monstrosities, which is quite unfair! I think these studies are extraordinary and very beautiful. I have enjoyed using similar motifs on several projects in the fruit and flower chapters and they make a refreshing alternative to pretty butterflies.*

Flower pots and insects are easy to find, but the sconce and the design on it may not be. However, you can quite easily find leaves and you could create your own insect and foliage design on the top of a box or around a tray, for instance. To give the projects an aged look, a burnt sienna glaze was added to the candle holder and sconce edging, then the panel was completed with a craquelure technique (see page 32).

How to achieve the look

Paint the flower pots in a muted colour of your choice. Paint the entire sconce with a coat of off-white paint. Leave to dry. Mix some burnt sienna acrylic paint with acrylic gel medium and a little water. Brush this around the edging and on the candle holder with a 6 mm ($^1/_2$ in) fitch brush, to provide a soft translucent layer of colour.

Follow the basic découpage techniques for both the flower pots and sconce (see page 19). Use the antiquing paint described on page 30 for the flower pots, then apply two coats of matt varnish over the last satin layer to finish. Complete the sconce by following the craquelure process described on page 32, and seal with a matt oil-based varnish.

Chapter 6

ANIMALS AND SEA LIFE

Native farm animals, Indian elephants, snakes, hares, fish and seashells have all played their part in creating this diverse range of découpaged designs.

Country Kitchen

I found these wonderful naïve animal designs on a range of greetings cards. The design was printed on both sides and, when fully opened, the animals were facing each other. The simple shapes combined with the orange and earthy red paint colours have made these some of my favourite projects in the book.

A variety of easy paint techniques was used on these projects; they were applied roughly and freely to help create a simple country look. The backing sheet on the cards was separated from the printed side. Because the card had a very glossy surface, the thinned print tended to curl and extra care was needed when gluing the edges down. They have an awkward habit of lifting up and a certain amount of persistence and re-gluing was required to keep them in their place.

How to achieve the look

Paint all the items on the outside with white satin latex. Paint the inside of the jug with red ochre paint and the inside of the planter a buff colour. Dilute some orange latex paint with water to make a wash of colour. Add some acrylic gel medium to slow down the drying time if you like. Brush this colour on to one of the projects with cross-hatched brush strokes, using a flat varnish brush. Dab a dishcloth over this to soften the effect. Paint the surface of the remaining projects in the same way. When dry, brush on a second coat of orange, this time leaving the brush marks visible.

Dilute some red ochre latex paint and brush this roughly over the buff paint on the inside of the planter. Using only one wash of colour gives a fairly patchy result, but this is intentional. Next, follow the basic découpage techniques to decorate all the projects (see page 19). Once these have been given two or three coats of varnish and allowed to dry, add the bands of contrasting colour to the now-protected orange surface.

Paint a dilute red ochre colour on to the top and bottom rim and the handles of the planter, using a narrow brush. Use masking tape to avoid smudging over the orange surface. Place a band of flexible masking tape around the edges of the bookend. Place a second strip inside this and remove the first one, which will leave you a straight, narrow edge. Paint the edges of the bookends with the same colour. Add the zigzag pattern to the jug after it has been découpaged and the orange paint is protected by the varnish. Start by drawing a freehand zigzag line with a pencil on the top and bottom edges of the jug. It doesn't matter if the zigzags are not even – this adds to the hand-painted look. Fill this in with green latex or acrylic paint, diluted as necessary. Distress this paint a little with fine-grade sandpaper. Continue varnishing all the projects, finishing with two coats of matt varnish.

INDIAN ELEPHANTS

*H*at boxes have a generous surface for decoration and this unusually-shaped set seems to have been tailor-made for the different-sized but similar elephant designs. Both designs were cut from giftwrap and the smaller box has a trail of elephants dancing around the lid. I have continued the oriental theme by using rich reds and gold, and by stencilling stars over the paint. You could découpage the gold stars by drawing the shapes on to gold paper, or even use the adhesive-backed stars that you can buy in packets from stationers.

The hat boxes were painted in slightly different reds that worked best with the colours in the cloths on the elephants' backs. A raspberry red was used for the larger box and a lacquer red for the small one. The gold bands and stars were added after the elephants were glued down and varnished.

How to achieve the look

Paint the hat boxes with two coats of red paint, then leave to dry thoroughly. Follow the basic découpage techniques for cutting, gluing and varnishing the designs (see page 19).

To paint the stripe around the edge of large lid, stipple gold acrylic colour on with a stencil brush so that it almost completely covers the red, but leaves some showing through in places. To paint the inner six-sided line on the lid of the smaller box, you need to mark the angles accurately with a water-soluble pencil. Draw three lines across the lid to connect each angle to the one opposite. You will now be able to use masking tape to define a border that has six equal sides. Mask a second border around the lid edge and, using a small paintbrush, paint both of these borders gold. Sponge off the pencil marks.

Look for stars that you can trace, or draw your own, to make a stencil with different-sized stars. They don't need to be absolutely accurate. Dip your stencil brush into gold acrylic paint, dab off the excess on to a piece of paper towel and stencil the gold stars on to the boxes. Put the large stars in place on the lid first and fill in the gaps with smaller ones. Varnish the boxes with two coats of matt varnish to complete.

WILD THINGS

A *brilliant brass stencil enabled me to produce the snake-skin effect on the papier mâché boxes, and the rich dark colours helped to create a realistic leathery effect. The curvy snake designs and the extraordinary shaped boxes made a perfect combination and could have been designed for each other. The paint-distressed wooden Shaker box with its hare motif completes this trio of unusual and masculine-looking designs. You can find plenty of similar natural history prints in books of copyright-free designs.*

How to achieve the look

Paint the snake boxes with two coats of paint. A mid-green colour was used for the green box and a reddish brown was used for the other one. Lightly mark a line down the centre of the box lid with a pencil. Place the stencil in position on one half of the box, lining up the start of the stencil with the drawn line. Dip a stencil brush into dark maroon acrylic paint (for the brown box; use a deep Hooker's green for the other one), wiping off the excess on a piece of paper towel so that very little paint remains. Stipple the stencil brush over the surface until you have completed the section. Line up the stencil to complete the area at the end of the box if necessary. Complete the other half of the lid in the same way and continue around the edges of the lid and the sides of the box.

Paint the hare box with two coats of rust-coloured paint, then brush one coat of dark blue paint over this. Rub a medium-grade sandpaper over the blue paint to reveal the rust colour beneath.

Take photocopies of your chosen natural history prints and stain them with tea to antique them (see page 27). Then follow the basic découpage techniques (see page 19) to complete the projects.

Applying paint through a brass stencil.

Bending the stencil to fit the curves.

LOAVES AND FISHES

I had this new enamel bread bin for ages and never seemed able to find cutouts suitable for its proportions or function. I haven't come across any prints of bread loaves, and wheat is far too difficult to cut out, but I do think this fish looks rather fine and quite appropriate for a kitchen. The fish on both these projects were hand-tinted nineteenth-century prints and it's interesting to see how two different treatments of similar prints can produce such contrasting results. The bread bin design incorporates some simple freehand painting on the lid and has a light fresh appearance, while the new tin dish has been decorated with earthy yellows and greens and given a heavily antiqued appearance.

How to achieve the look

BREAD BIN

Paint the outside of the bread bin off-white, leaving the inside unpainted. Mix some yellow ochre and a touch of raw umber acrylic paint with acrylic gel medium and a little water. Sponge this over the off-white paint to achieve a soft, even texture. Leave to dry for about four hours. Mix some ultramarine blue with some acrylic gel medium and water and paint the handle, then paint a fine line around the edge of the lid. Using a fine pointed brush, draw a few freehand circles on the lid. Follow the basic découpage techniques to complete (see page 19).

TIN DISH

Paint the inside of the dish with olive green and the outside with yellow ochre latex paint. Paint a green border around the tip of the dish using masking tape to protect the yellow paint. Follow the basic découpage techniques (see page 19) and use the antiquing paint technique on page 30 on the inside of the dish. Decorate the outside of the dish with the water-based crackle technique as described on page 88, and complete the ageing process by applying a yellowing antique wax.

SEASHELLS

*T*he scallop shell is a favourite motif of mine and its simple shape has appealed to designers for thousands of years. Shells are frequently used to decorate bathroom mirrors and frames, as they are perfect for creating a border around a frame. I have chosen to decorate some small wooden bathroom accessories using shell-pink and aquamarine colours to continue the seashell theme. The items are all made from soft balsa wood, which has quite a pronounced grain; a liming paste was worked into this to produce pretty textured pastel shades.

The shell prints I used are coloured etchings by George Sowerby and were first published in 1852. It is fairly easy to find shell illustrations in books and on sheets of giftwrap. You can buy water-based liming paste from specialist decorating suppliers. Do not confuse this with liming wax, as you cannot découpage on to a waxed surface.

How to achieve the look

To colour the wood, you can use either water-based pastel-coloured wood stain or diluted latex paint. The finished results look much the same with either product but the wood stain is more durable. This makes no difference once varnished, but on the soap dish, which must be left unvarnished, this is the more practical option. Apricot-coloured wood stain was used for the pink colour and diluted latex paint for the turquoise shade. Paint or stain your projects with your chosen colours and leave to dry thoroughly before decorating further.

Open up the grain in the wood on the exterior surfaces of the projects by rubbing them with a wire brush in the direction of the grain. Apply the liming paste evenly over the surface with a brush and leave this to dry.

Remove the excess paste from the surface with 00-grade steel wool, leaving behind the paste in the opened grain.

Arrange the shells evenly around the bottom of the wooden jar. Look at the space left between the shells and position them so that they fit together, leaving a narrow gap in between. Use repositional adhesive to hold them in place. Complete the projects following the instructions for the basic découpage techniques (see page 19), ending with two coats of matt varnish.

Removing liming paste with steel wool.

Close-up of the limed surface.

Chapter 7

CHILDREN'S WORLD

With contemporary, Victorian and traditional designs to choose from, there are ideas and designs to suit all ages of children, and perhaps some young-at-heart adults too!

CLOWNING AROUND

*C*hildren will love this knick-knack chest with little drawers to keep their trea-
sured possessions in. Clowns are always appealing to children and, although
the ones used here are from sheets of Victorian scraps, they have been given a
modern appearance by using bright red and cream colours and stencilled
spots. Clowns making faces are an amusing decoration for a child's mirror.
Have the children see if they can make the same faces in it!

The knick-knack chest was coloured
with water-based wood stains and I
used matching latex and acrylic paint
colours on the mirror frame. Water-
based red wood stain is fairly easy to
find and it colours and seals a
surface in one application. Cream
wood stain is less commonly
available and I used it because it was
to hand – but you can replace it with
diluted latex paint for an equally
successful result.

How to achieve the look

Remove the drawers and paint the
outside of the chest with red wood
stain. This area is now completed.

Colour the drawer fronts with wood
stain or diluted latex paint.

Brush two coats of cream latex paint
over the frame. I worked out an
arrangement of evenly-spaced dots
that fitted around the frame and I cut
a stencil to fit the design. This isn't
strictly necessary – simply paint the
dots where you like. Paint or stencil
dots over the frame in red acrylic
paint, using either a fine-pointed
artist's brush or a stencil brush as
appropriate. If you wish, you can do
this after the clowns have been glued
in position. Follow the basic
découpage techniques (see page 19)
to complete the projects.

TOYTOWN

I have used this children's giftwrap more often than any other and I can't count the number of my students who have used this paper to decorate place mats for children. The old-fashioned toy motifs have a nostalgic appeal to adults and they lend themselves very well to projects where you require an aged appearance. The designs are printed on brown wrapping paper, so the brown paper lampshade provided a particularly suitable base for the cutouts. The lamp base and miniature bucket were antiqued using a wax resist paint finish.

If you are unable to find a brown paper lampshade, you could back some brown wrapping paper with a piece of card and re-cover an old shade. I glued the motifs in place on the shade with a spray adhesive, so that the brown paper was not marked, which would have shown up very clearly when the lamp was switched on! The base was a plain wooden chain store purchase painted the same colours as the toys.

How to achieve the look

Paint the bucket and the lamp base with two coats of red paint. When this is dry, apply some clear liquid wax to the lamp base and the outside of the bucket with a small brush. Place it in areas where you want the red to show through, particularly on the edges and other areas where the paint would naturally wear. Use a stencil brush to flick some spots of wax on the surface here and there. Leave this to dry for at least half an hour, then paint some dark blue paint over this. When this is dry, rub 00-grade steel wool over the surface, which will remove some of the blue paint where the wax was applied.

Use the basic découpage techniques (see page 19) to complete the decoration of the bucket, then brush two or three coats of varnish over the lamp base for protection. Allow to dry thoroughly.

Arrange the cutout motifs on the paper shade, using repositional adhesive to keep them in place. When you are happy with the arrangement, remove one motif at a time, spray the back of the cutout with permanent spray adhesive suitable for craft work and stick the motif back down on the shade. I left the shade unvarnished but you can decide whether or not you want to varnish it.

PLAYTIME

I was delighted to find a giftwrap which was decorated with the characters from the children's classic story Alice in Wonderland. *The figures had the advantage of being well-defined and easy to cut out. The idea for the yellow stripes on the background of the toy chest came from the paper itself. Teddy bears gaze reassuringly from the hanging wall plaque.*

How to achieve the look

Paint the chest with two or three coats of white latex paint, using a paint roller. Decide on the width of stripes that you require. Use a ruler and pencil to mark the centre of the lid with a series of vertical dots. Position the first stripe in the middle of this line. Mark the width of the stripes with a dot, starting from the middle of the centre and working towards each edge. Mark a second and third horizontal row on each side of this line towards the edges of the lid. You will now have three rows of dots, both horizontally and vertically. Continue marking the sides of the chest in the same way. Place a piece of masking tape on each side of the middle stripe and alternate stripes

thereafter. You can use a continuous strip of tape up one side, over the lid and down the other.

Apply the yellow paint with a roller between the masked areas, then remove the tape. When the paint is dry, sand the surface with fine-grade finishing paper so as not to scratch the paint.

Paint the teddy bear plaque eggshell blue. Brush a slightly diluted coat of turquoise paint around the moulded edges, so that the lighter colour is still visible beneath it. Complete both projects following the basic découpage techniques (see page 19), then apply a matt varnish to finish.

NOAH'S ARK

I loved using these stunning contemporary Noah's Ark giftwraps and have almost completely covered the projects with them. The charming, rather wobbly borders from the wrapping paper play a very important part in the designs. The cupboard and large toy bin may look as if they have been covered with a large, continuous sheet of paper, but in fact they were decorated with different sections of paper that were linked with a colourful border. Put together two sheets of terrific giftwrap, a cheap metal wastepaper bin, a 25cm (10in) square of fibreboard, photocopied numbers and a clock movement, and you will be able to create these eye-catching designs on a shoestring budget.

The square of fibreboard will need a hole drilled in the centre to accommodate the clock movement. Because the paint colour is only seen on the top and bottom rims of the wastepaper bin and around the edges of the clock, there is no need to paint the whole of these items, just the parts on view. There are gaps between the borders on the other two projects, so you will need to paint all of these. You will find a lino printing roller a really useful piece of equipment for smoothing out air bubbles and flattening the paper.

How to achieve the look

TOY BUCKET AND CUPBOARD

Paint the cupboard and tall toy bucket a deep blue. The bucket will need to be decorated one side at a time and the paper has to be trimmed to fit the curved surface. Place the central part of the design on the bucket, using repositional adhesive to hold it in place. Draw a vertical line down the halfway mark on each side of the bucket, over the paper. Place the tip of a pencil in the centre of the top edge of the design. Rest your arm on a support and, keeping your hand still, rotate the bucket so that a horizontal line is drawn on the surface. It is easier if someone helps you. Mark a similar horizontal line around the bottom of the design.

Remove the design and trim away the paper that does not fall within the marked lines. Glue this in place and continue adding other border designs in varying widths until you have covered most of the surface. The narrower borders can be stretched to fit and don't need trimming. Repeat the design on the other side and place a border down each side of the bucket to cover the area where the two sides join.

The flat surface of the cupboard is simpler to decorate. Arrange the design and borders on the cupboard so that the surface is almost covered, then glue in place. Complete with three or more coats of acrylic varnish.

WASTEPAPER CAN AND CLOCK

Paint the clock edges and the top and bottom of the wastepaper can bright turquoise, and the inside of the can with dark brown paint. Glue the design around the middle of the can first, then add the border to the top and bottom. Cut a square of wrapping paper to cover the clock. Add a small Noah's Ark motif in the centre of the square, then glue on the fish border and mitre the corners as described on page 16. The bottom border needs the central section cut from the rest and turned around so that the fish are not swimming upside down! Cut out the photocopied numbers and paint them with India ink to blacken them. Glue these in place and finish with three or more coats of varnish.

Chapter 8

TREASURE TROVE

inally, take some oriental embroidery, Chinese cut-paper designs, pietre dure, *golden musical instruments, old advertising cuts, letters and playing cards, and combine these with exciting background papers and paint effects to create some amazing and beautiful designs.*

ORIENTAL EMBROIDERY

There are many beautiful giftwraps decorated with embroidery and tapestry designs. These designs are often very intricate and considerable patience is needed in cutting and arranging them. But your finished projects will have an elegant and timeless quality and, who knows, they may even become the antiques of tomorrow.

The fabric lampshade came from a chain store and I was fortunate to find one with a trim that colour-matched the embroidery motifs so well. The lamp base had already been painted, but if you want to decorate a glazed ceramic surface you will need to paint it first with a primer. The lampshade needs to be sealed, glued and re-sealed with the same glue throughout to prevent a patchy appearance on the fabric.

How to achieve the look

Paint the lamp base and box with a stone-coloured paint and the tray a dark blue. Cut out a variety of motifs and experiment with different arrangements. The flowers and tree blossom on the tray need to be assembled from different elements of the design and more or less reinvented. Follow the basic découpage techniques (see page 19) for all these projects, then finish with a matt varnish. Complete the tray with dark brown wax. Rub or brush gilt cream on the rim, choosing a colour that is complementary to the russet shades in the paper.

Seal the lampshade with white glue. Follow the basic découpage instructions (see page 19) but use white glue, not paste, and seal the glued design with white glue as well. You can varnish the shade on top of the glue, but do not apply more than three layers or it might crack.

PRECIOUS STONES

An absolutely stunning pietre dure *giftwrap design was used to decorate this lovely old cutlery box and chess board. The paper is also very versatile, providing large motifs for the top of the box, and tiny pieces for the edge of the chess board. The delicate trailing vines formed a border around the wrapping paper edges; the same design was used for a very different look on the tray and wine carrier on page 78. The chess board was made from a 45 cm (18 in) square of fibreboard and cost practically nothing.*

The chess board has alternate gilded squares with an attractive textured appearance. This was the result of a happy accident when I found that no matter how low-tack the masking tape was, it always lifted fragments of shellac, even varnished shellac, from the gilded surface. The simple solution was to even the effect and use the low-tack tape to lift the varnish in the same way from the gilded squares or parts of squares that had not been affected. The cutlery box was given a gold painted border to frame the motifs on the lid and pull the elements together.

How to achieve the look

Paint the chess board with a plum-coloured paint using a paint roller, then paint a 2.5 cm (1 in) black border around the edge using masking tape. When this is dry, put masking tape over the border and give the rest of the board a coat of off-white latex paint, again using the paint roller. When this is dry, rub the surface with a fine-grade sandpaper to reveal patches of the underlying paint colour. Seal the surface with acrylic varnish.

With a pencil and ruler, mark horizontal and vertical lines spaced 5 cm (2 in) apart. Place a strip of low-tack masking tape on each side of alternate horizontal and vertical lines. Gild these squares following the basic gilding technique on page 28. Brush a coat of dark shellac over each square to tone down the bright gold leaf,

then seal each square with acrylic varnish. Peel off the tape, then mask the remaining squares in the same way and repeat the process until you have gilded all the alternate squares. Remove all the masking tape from the board. Stick a new strip of low-tack tape over areas that haven't been affected by removing the tape, then lift it off immediately, to even up the textured effect. Seal the board with three coats of acrylic varnish, allowing each coat to dry before applying the next.

Paint the cutlery box black. When dry, mask off a border round the edges of the box lid and paint this with gold acrylic paint. Follow the basic découpage techniques (see page 19) to complete both designs, finishing with a coat of matt varnish and allow to dry thoroughly.

THEMES AND VARIATIONS

*I*t is appropriate to extend the découpage process by pasting your designs on to cut paper backgrounds. If it is playing about with paper rather than messing about with paint that appeals, then this could be the approach for you. There is no shortage of colours and textures to choose from and you can create your own by photocopying old documents, manuscripts, music and even a newspaper typographical collage. Newspaper itself yellows, but it photocopies well. Unfortunately, I haven't room to show all these ideas on just two pages, but I hope you will be inspired to have a go.

Look for appropriate papers to cover your projects. The items illustrated were decorated as follows. The music on the front of the case was copied from a book of piano music, while the decoration around the top and sides as well as the motifs, came from a copyright-free book of music designs. The background papers on the card boxes are giftwrap and the playing cards were cut from a book of card designs. A pack of cards would be too thick to use, but you could photocopy them and use the photocopies instead. A snakeskin-textured paper and a subtle hand-marbled one were used for the letters box. The letters and nibs were cut from a piece of giftwrap, but you could use old postcards.

How to achieve the look

Refer to the technique for covering a book box on page 24, and use it for covering the music case as well as the card boxes. Cut out or photocopy appropriate motifs. If you require an antique look, your chosen papers can be aged by staining with tea (see page 27). The case is fairly large, which requires joining together several lengths of paper. Smaller pieces will need to be joined on the top to accommodate the clasps and handle. You can overlap the paper as you like. Cover the front and back of the case first, then the top, bottom and sides.

Follow the basic découpage techniques (see page 19) to complete all the projects. The book boxes can be left unvarnished and given a ribbon tie if you prefer a natural look, although varnish will protect the decoration.

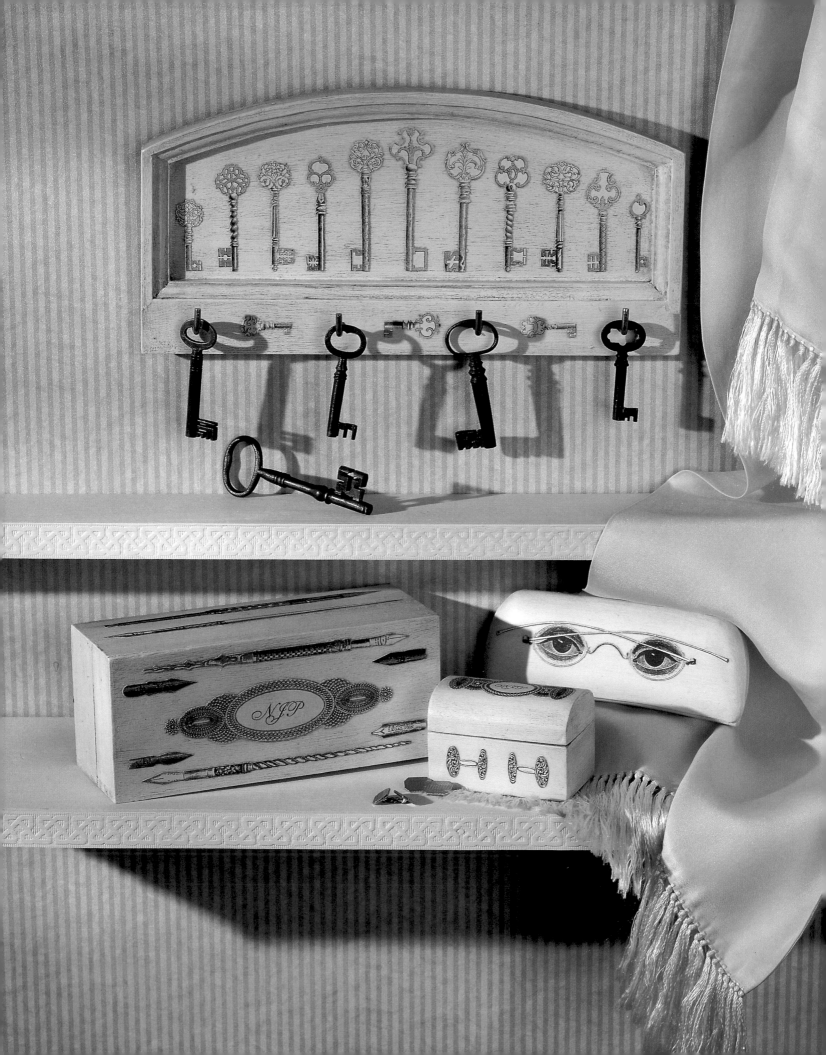

REMEMBER ME

I like to decorate items with motifs that indicate their use. Although this is an obvious device, it is not particularly easy to buy things that use it. Apart from the keys, which I found in a book of historical ornament, all the cutouts were photocopied from early household and jewellery catalogues. You can find reproductions of these catalogues quite easily and they contain delightful illustrations. I photocopied the designs in various colours on to a cream-coloured paper and painted the background the same colour. This gives the illusion that the designs have been printed on the surfaces.

You will need to use a photocopier that can scan colour. Ask for a colour chart and choose a dark colour. Black-and-white prints do not transfer very well to light shades and lack strength of colour. I wanted a deep dusky pink but apparently this can be a difficult colour. Often the result is a choice between orange-red, red-brown or magenta, so if you are paying for each mistake, you have been warned! The dark blue, green and brown shades were not a problem. I printed the monograms using a typeface on my computer, added ornamental surrounds, then colour-copied these like the rest.

How to achieve the look

Look for appropriate prints and items that you can put together. Colour-copy them in the colour of your choice on to cream-coloured paper, enlarging or reducing the size if necessary. Choose a paint colour to match the copy paper and paint all your projects with this colour. Follow the basic découpage techniques (see page 19) for all the projects. Apply matt varnish, then antique the items with brown wax.

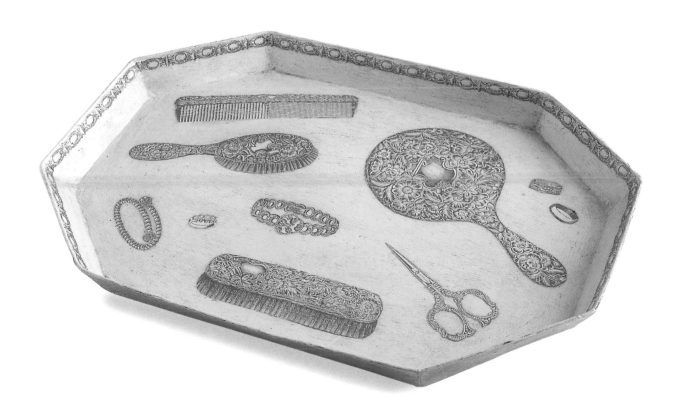

SILHOUETTES

here are many books of silhouettes to choose from, and while some designs are charming they do not suit all tastes. I discovered a book of Chinese folk designs which was based on a collection of cut-paper designs. These are absolutely brilliant and provide a beautiful range of simple silhouette shapes that are easily cut out. What's more, this copyright-free book of designs is just as easily obtainable as those previously mentioned. I gilded the back of photocopied images and used a lacquered effect for the table, to continue the oriental theme. The tortoiseshell frame contains a more traditional silhouette image and this has been placed on a piece of gilded card.

How to achieve the look

TABLE

Paint the table with two or three coats of a lacquer-red paint. Seal this with two coats of acrylic varnish. Apply a little black acrylic paint here and there over the surface with a fine artist's brush, especially in areas where you want the lacquer to look worn such as edges and other areas where you would normally expect wear. Using a piece of paper towel or soft cloth, spread and remove some of the paint to create a realistic effect that doesn't look too splodgy.

Photocopy your silhouette images. Gild the paper on the reverse of the printed side, following the instructions on page 28. Seal the gilded surface with shellac. Follow the basic découpage techniques (see page 19) to complete the projects. Finally, brush brown shellac over the surface to give an aged appearance, then seal with acrylic varnish.

FRAME

Paint the frame with lacquer-red paint, then seal the surface with two coats of acrylic varnish. Add a teaspoon of sugar to half a cup of vinegar and mix well. Take a teaspoonful each of burnt umber and black powdered pigment and add enough of the vinegar mix to make a thin but opaque paint. Section off two diagonally opposite ends of the frame with masking tape, then paint the vinegar paint on the other two corners. Gather a length of damp chamois leather, or cotton rag, into a sausage shape and roll this over the wet paint. Use a softening brush to disperse some of the paint. Repeat on the remaining corners, this time

rolling the leather or rag in the other direction. Seal with acrylic varnish.

Photocopy decorative motifs for the frame on to acetate and gild the acetate and a piece of card to fit inside the frame, following the instructions on page 28. Cut out the acetate motifs and glue them on the frame with white glue. Cut out a silhouette and blacken the image with India ink. Glue this in place on the card using the same glue. Seal both the frame and the picture with three or more coats of acrylic varnish. Finally, brush a coat of dark shellac over both the frame and picture, and seal with acrylic varnish.

Rolling a bunched rag over wet paint.

MUSICAL MALACHITE

I complete this book by interpreting a concept that inspired me when I first thought about writing on new ideas about découpage – Fornasetti's malachite plates with golden musical instruments. Ideas cannot always be successfully transformed into reality, and this is particularly true with découpage which relies so heavily on found images. This tray is exactly as I had planned. The shape lends itself particularly well to the malachite effect, which was produced by dividing the tray into manageable areas and dragging a piece of torn card through a wet acrylic glaze in each area.

How to achieve the look

A very smooth surface is required for the malachite paint finish to work and you need to ensure that you do not have adjacent wet surfaces. You can find the musical instruments in copyright-free design books.

Paint the tray with turquoise paint, using the colour in the photograph below as a guide. Divide the tray into sections by laying a long ruler or straight edge over two opposite angles and drawing a line with a pencil between them. Repeat with all the angles so that the tray is divided into eight segments. Continue drawing this line by eye, up the inside of the tray, over the top rim and down the outside. Mark the octagonal centre section by drawing

horizontal lines between the segments an equal distance from the edge. Mask around this section with low-tack tape and paint it first.

Mix some viridian green and a little raw umber acrylic paint with acrylic gel medium and paint a generous coating randomly over the surface. Stipple the glaze with a stencil brush to even out the texture. Take a piece of card torn from a cereal box or something similar and run it over the wet glaze, wiggling and curving it as you do so, to form the patterned effect. Do not leave the glaze too long or it will start to dry and become unworkable. Remove the masking tape and let this portion dry before proceeding. Mask the octagonal centre

with low-tack tape and place a strip on the outside of each alternate segment. Complete these four segments in the same way, wiping away any paint smudges. When these are dry, repeat the process on the other four sections, then on the tray sides.

Remove all the masking tape and, using a fine-pointed brush, add additional lines of colour here and there, strengthening other lines and generally tidying up the appearance. Using the same brush, define the lines between the sections.

Photocopy pictures of musical instruments on to acetate and gild the acetate following the technique on page 28. Cut them out and glue them on to the tray with white glue. Complete the tray by varnishing with ten or more coats of acrylic varnish.

Stippling paint with a stencil brush.

Dragging torn card over the wet glaze.

SUPPLIERS

Paper sources

Artifacts Inc
PO Box 3399
Palestine
TX 75801
Tel: 903-729-4178
Fax: 903-723-3903
*Call for stockists of Mamelok Press
Victorian scraps*

Caspari Ltd
Catalog mail order: 1-800-CASPARI
Giftwraps, cards

Dover Bookstore
180 Varrick Street
9th Floor
New York
NY 10014
Tel: 212-255-6399
Catalog mail order: 516-294-7000
Copyright-free design books

Kate's Paperie
541 Broadway
New York
NY 10012
Tel: 212-941-9816
Catalog mail order: 1-800-809-9880
*Store has large collection of giftwraps
Mail-order catalog has limited
selection of giftwraps and some crafts
materials*

Kensington Cards Inc
505 S. Beverly Drive #1411
Beverly Hills
CA 90212
Tel: 310-839-2440
Fax: 310-839-2449
*Call for stockists of National Gallery
giftwraps*

The National Trust (Enterprises) Ltd
PO Box 101
Melksham
Wiltshire SN12 8EA
UK
Tel: +44-1225-790800
Fax: +44-1225-792269
*Print room border sheets; call for
details of mail-order service*

Notes and Queries
PO Box 18426
Baltimore
MD 21237
Tel: 410-682-6102
Fax: 410-682-5397
*Call for stockists of Roger la Borde
giftwrap in the United States*

Past Times
Suite 400
100 Cummings Center
Beverly
MA 01915-6102
Catalog mail order: 1-800-621-6020
Victorian scraps by mail order

Porter Design
38 Anacapa Street
Santa Barbara
CA 93101
Tel: 805-568-5433
Fax: 805-568-5435
*Fine art prints (Classical Dancers on
page 38)*

Roger la Borde
87 Kingsgate Road
West Hampstead
London NW6 4JY
UK
Tel: +44-171-328-0491
Fax: +44-171-372-5145
e-mail:
rogerlaborde@compuserve.com
*Contemporary giftwrap, including
designs on pages 64–9 and 126–7*

B. Shackman & Co
83 Fifth Avenue
New York
NY 10002
Tel: 212-989-5162
Fax: 212-242-3832
*Victorian scraps, mail-order catalog
available*

Blanks for decorating

Colour Blue
Beckhaven House
9 Gilbert Road
London SE11 5AA
UK
Tel: +44-171-820-7700
Fax: +44-171-793-0537
*Mail-order catalog with galvanized
metalware, including watering cans,
jugs, flower buckets, wall planters
and trays*

Crate & Barrel
650 Madison Avenue
New York
NY 10022
Tel: 212-308-0011
Fax: 212-644-7043
*Tissue holders, water jugs, bins, spice
racks, and other items available
through mail-order catalog*

The Decorative Arts Co Ltd
5A Royal Crescent
London W11 4SL
UK
Tel: +44-171-371-4303
Fax: +44-171-602-9189
*Papier mâché items, including hat
boxes, tissue boxes and bins; also
fibreboard frames, book boxes, wall
clocks, and other items by mail order*

Hold Everything
1311 Second Avenue
New York
NY 10021
Tel: 212-535-9446
Fax: 212-396-3332
Catalog mail order: 1-800-421-2264
Company occasionally carries plain wood boxes in various sizes

IKEA
Customer information and catalog:
East of Mississippi 1-800-434-4532
West of Mississippi 410-931-8940
Some unfinished wood items including desk accessories, pencil cups, storage boxes in various styles, and picture frames

Pottery Barn
1965 Broadway
New York, NY 10023
Tel: 212-579-8477
Fax: 212-579 8460
Catalog mail order 1-800-922-5507
Bins, tissue holders, trays, vases, and other items by mail order

Scumble Goosie
Lewiston Mill
Toadsmore Road
Brimscombe
Stroud
Gloucestershire GL5 2TB
UK

Tel: +44-1453-731305
Fax: +44-1453-731500
Fibreboard/wooden furniture, screens, umbrella stands, letter racks, and more by mail order

Somerset Creative Products
Laurel Farm
Westham
Wedmore
Somerset BS28 4UZ
UK
Tel: +44-1934-712416
Fax: +44-1934-712210
Unpainted wooden country items, including garden carriers, trays, wine carriers, and herb boxes

Other suppliers

Gracious Home
1220 Third Avenue
New York
NY 10021
Tel: 212-517-6300
Fax: 212-249-1534
Large collection of stencils, crafts materials, no mail-order catalog, phone orders accepted, world-wide shipping available

Pearl
308 Canal Street
New York
NY 10013-2572
Tel: 212-431-7932
Fax: 212-431-5420
Catalog mail order: 1-800-221-6845 ext. 2297
Gilt creams, coloured waxes, rottenstone, raw umber pigment, crackle varnish, acrylic gel medium, shellac, metal leaf, acrylic gold size, acrylic varnish, acrylic glaze, drying agents and special brushes. Mail order available

Vanguard Crafts Inc
1081 East 48th Street
Brooklyn
NY 11234
Tel: 718-377-5188
Fax: 718-692-0056
Catalog mail order: 1-800-662-7238
Arts and crafts materials, catalog available

ACKNOWLEDGEMENTS

A big thank you to Kit for her brilliant styling and understanding, to David for his terrific pics and to Heather for coming to the rescue. Very many thanks also to Sheila at Aurum for saying yes, without hesitation, when I first suggested this book, and to Joan and Hilary for their invaluable help with cutting out

and painting. Special thanks to Nick for his encouragement, being a wiz with the PC, and for his patient and considered responses to my endless requests for his opinion.

I would also like to acknowledge the following illustrators for their paper designs:

Julie Arkell for the design on page 65 for Roger La Borde © 1989; Jacqueline Mair for designs on page 64 for Roger La Borde © 1991 and 1994, pages 66–7 for Roger La Borde © 1995, and on pages 68–9 for Roger La Borde © 1995; and Jane Ray for designs on pages 126–7 for Roger La Borde © 1991.